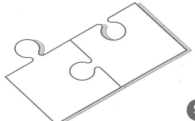

LOUIS FIDGE

essential
English

Book 4

STANLEY
THORNES

Acknowledgements

The author and publishers wish to thank the following
for permission to use copyright material.

Carcanet Press Ltd for Edwin Morgan, 'The Loch Ness Monster's Song'
from *Collected Poems*.

Laura Cecil Literary Agency on behalf of the James Reeves Estate
for James Reeves, 'Giant Thunder' from *Complete Poems for Children*, Heinemann.

Encyclopedia Britannica, Inc for an extract from the Index,
'Mandarin Duck' – 'Manet' of *Children's Britannica*.
Copyright © 1975 by Encyclopedia Britannica, Inc.

Wes Magee for his poem 'The House on the Hill'. Copyright © Wes Magee.

Oxford University Press for an extract, 'Dahl, Roald' from
Oxford Children's Encyclopedia, Vol. 6.

Rogers, Coleridge & White Ltd on behalf of the author for Gareth Owen,
'Winter Days' from *Salford Road and Other Poems*, 1988, Young Lions.
Copyright © Gareth Owen 1988.

Walker Books Ltd for material from Marcia Williams,
Greek Myths for Young Children. Copyright © 1991 by Marcia Williams.

Every effort has been made to trace all the copyright holders,
but if any have been overlooked, the publishers will be pleased
to make the necessary arrangements at the first opportunity.

First published in 1996 by
Stanley Thornes (Publishers) Ltd
Ellenborough House
Wellington Street
Cheltenham GL50 1YW

96 97 98 99 00 / 10 9 8 7 6 5 4 3 2 1

A catalogue record for this book is available from the British Library.

ISBN 0 7487 2541 5

Design and typesetting by Brian Green Associates.
Illustration by Claire Boyce, Jeffrey Burn, Tony Dover, Virginia Gray, Kyle Green,
Mandy Lillywhite, Malcolm Livingstone, Tony O'Donnell, Dandi Palmer and Kay Whiteman.

Printed in Hong Kong.

CONTENTS

Something very strange was happening to Treehorn. The first thing he noticed was that he couldn't reach the shelf in his closet that he had always been able to reach before, the one where he hid his candy bars and bubble gum. Then he noticed his trousers were getting too big.

'My trousers are all stretching or something,' said Treehorn to his mother. 'I'm tripping on them all the time.'

'That's too bad, dear,' said his mother, looking in the oven. 'I do hope this cake isn't going to fall,' she said.

'And my sleeves come down way below my hands,' said Treehorn. 'So my shirts must be stretching too.'

'Think of that,' said Treehorn's mother.

'I just don't know why this cake isn't rising the way it should. Mrs Abernale's cakes are always nice. They always rise.'

Treehorn started out of the kitchen. He tripped on his trousers, which indeed did seem to be getting longer and longer.

At dinner that night Treehorn's father said, 'Do sit up, Treehorn. I can hardly see your head.'

'I am sitting up,' said Treehorn. 'This is as far up as I come. I think I must be shrinking or something.'

'I'm sorry the cake didn't turnout very well,' said Treehorn's mother.

'It's very nice, dear,' said Treehorn's father politely.

Florence Parry Heide

> It is important to begin stories in an interesting way.
> Look at how the opening paragraph makes you want to read on!

COMPREHENSION

● Starting points ●

Choose the correct answer for each question and write it in your book.

1 Treehorn couldn't reach the shelf in his
   a) cupboard   **b)** wardrobe   **c)** closet

2 In his closet Treehorn hid his
   a) pens   **b)** bubble gum   **c)** torch

3 Treehorn thought his trousers were
   a) shrinking   **b)** stretching   **c)** smelling

4 Treehorn's mother was making
   a) a cake   **b)** some bread   **c)** dinner

5 Whose cakes were always nice?
   a) Mrs Allen's   **b)** Mrs Arthur's   **c)** Mrs Abernale's

6 Treehorn's father told him to
   a) sit up   **b)** stand up   **c)** shut up

> **extra**
> See what you can find out about Lewis Carroll's book called 'Alice in Wonderland'.

4

● Moving on ●

A dictionary may be used for checking spellings and for finding the meanings of words.

1 Which words in the passage show the book was written by an American?

2 What can you learn about Treehorn's parents from the passage?

3 What sort of problems would you have if you shrunk?

4 List some good things about being very small?

STUDY SKILLS

● Using a dictionary ●

Use a dictionary to help you write these words correctly.

1 a) Australian animal –   kan____ _____

   b) hair grown on upper lip –   mous_____

   c) to make someone feel awkward –   emb_____

   d) to taste lovely –   del_____

   e) thief –   bur_____

shhh!

Write what you think the meanings of these words are.
Do not use a dictionary!

2 a) mountain   **b)** shield   **c)** pilot   **d)** explorer   **e)** destroy

3 Now use a dictionary to check the meanings you wrote for the words in question 2. Rewrite any you are not happy with.

Look up and find two different meanings for each of these words.
Write them in your book.

4 a) tear   **b)** fire   **c)** bowl   **d)** row   **e)** watch

extra

Look up and write the meanings of these words:

   camouflage

   chaos

   symphony

   evacuate

   atrocious

   lagoon

WORD STUDY

● Growing words ●

Match each adjective with the root word from which it has grown.
Write the pairs of words in your book like this:

root words	adjectives
music	musical

extra

Now make each adjective into an adverb like this:

musical –
  musically

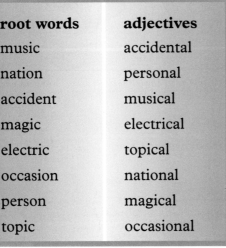

root words	adjectives
music	accidental
nation	personal
accident	musical
magic	electrical
electric	topical
occasion	national
person	magical
topic	occasional

● Root words ●

Copy out these words in your book. Underline the smaller root word in each from which the word has grown.

dangerous   unknown

darkness   signal

horizontal   safely

magician   noticeable

following

LANGUAGE STUDY

● Same words but different meanings! ●

Below, the word 'light' is used in three different ways:

1   as a noun

I switch on the <u>light</u>.

2   as a verb

I <u>light</u> a fire.

3   as an adjective

I pick up a <u>light</u> weight.

In these sentences a noun has been underlined. Make up another sentence and use that word as a verb. Do it like this:

    I had a <u>drink</u>.   Please <u>drink</u> all your milk.

1 a) I broke my <u>watch</u>.

   b) It was a long <u>race</u>.

   c) The <u>fly</u> was stuck in the web.

   d) The <u>smoke</u> made me cough.

   e) My mum has a lovely gold <u>ring</u>.

   f) I went to the top of the building in the <u>lift</u>.

In these sentences an adjective has been underlined. Make up another sentence and use that word as a noun. Do it like this:

    Mum gave me a <u>cold</u> orange juice.   I got wet and caught a <u>cold</u>.

2 a) The <u>iron</u> gate fell off its hinges.

   b) I squashed the <u>paper</u> cup.

   c) The sculptor carved the <u>stone</u> statue skilfully.

   d) His <u>fat</u> dog became exhausted.

   e) The <u>play</u> area was full of children.

   f) I drew a <u>round</u> shape in the sand.

(i) **Remember**

A **noun** is a name of a person, place or thing.

A **verb** is a 'doing' or 'being' word.

An **adjective** is a describing word which tells us more about a noun.

extra

*Make up some sentences and show how you could use the words below as a **verb** and an **adjective**.*

clean

wet

coloured

lead

WRITING WORKSHOP

● Thinking about stories ●

Use this ladder to help you think about story planning.

STEP 4 - STORYLINE (PLOT)

Beginning
• Can you make it interesting?

Middle
• What sort of things will happen?

Ending
• Will it be happy?   • sad?
• exciting?   • interesting?

STEP 3 - CHARACTERS

Who will the main characters be?
• human? • animals?
• others (like robots, space creatures etc.)?

What will they be like?
• How will they look?
• What personalities will they have?
• What will they say and do?

STEP 2 - SETTING

When will it take place?
• in the present (now)?
• in the future (in time to come)?
• in the past (in time gone by)?

Where will it take place?
• in a real place (like a house, tent, castle)?
• in an imaginary place (underwater, space)?

STEP 1 - TYPE OF STORY

What type of story will it be?
• adventure?   • animal?
• funny?   • frightening?
• real life?   • imaginary?
• some other type?

Start at the
bottom of
the ladder.

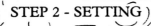 **AUDIENCE**

You also need
to think about who
you are writing the
story for. It might
be:

just for you;

your friends;

for younger
children;

for older readers;

for people you
have never met.

8

Thinking about
● 'The Shrinking of Treehorn' ●

Read 'The Shrinking of Treehorn' on page 4 again.

Answer these questions in your book.

1 What type of story do you think it is?

    a) a war story? **b**) a horror story? **c**) a funny story

    d) an imaginary story? **e**) a space story?

2 Think about the setting. When does it take place?

    a) in the present? **b**) the future? **c**) the past?

3 Where does it take place?

    a) in a town? **b**) in the country? **c**) in a cave?

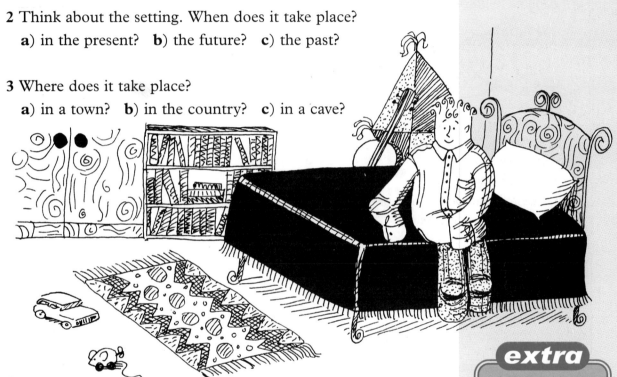

4 What do you think Treehorn's bedroom was like?
Write a description.

5 Think about the characters.
Write a description of what you think Treehorn was like.
Say what he looked like, what he wore. Say what sort of boy
he was. Explain what thoughts would have been going
through his mind when he discovered he was shrinking. How
would he have felt?

6 Think about the plot.
The passage on page 4 is the very beginning of the book.
Treehorn eventually becomes very small and has some very
funny adventures. Think of some of the amusing things that
could have happened to him. Write your own story called
'The Adventures of Treehorn'.

extra

*1 Write a letter
to Treehorn.*

*What sort of
questions will
you ask him?*

*2 Write from
another point of
view.*

*Write your own
version of the
opening of the
story from
Treehorn's mum's
point of view!*

Fast feats

Some animals need to be able to move quickly, to hunt prey or to escape when being hunted.

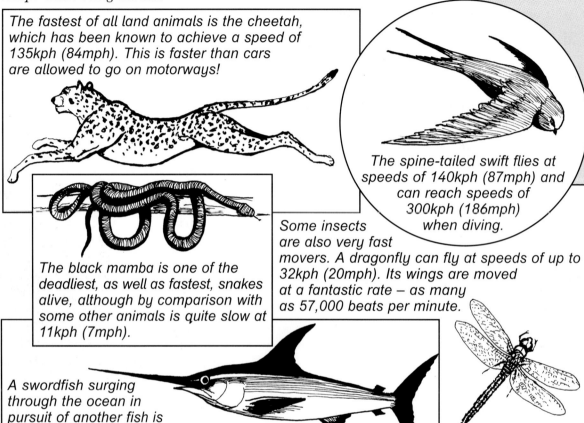

The fastest of all land animals is the cheetah, which has been known to achieve a speed of 135kph (84mph). This is faster than cars are allowed to go on motorways!

The spine-tailed swift flies at speeds of 140kph (87mph) and can reach speeds of 300kph (186mph) when diving.

The black mamba is one of the deadliest, as well as fastest, snakes alive, although by comparison with some other animals is quite slow at 11kph (7mph).

Some insects are also very fast movers. A dragonfly can fly at speeds of up to 32kph (20mph). Its wings are moved at a fantastic rate – as many as 57,000 beats per minute.

A swordfish surging through the ocean in pursuit of another fish is quite a sight. Swordfish can reach more than 90kph (56mph).

COMPREHENSION

● Starting points ●

Write in your book true, false *or* can't tell *for each statement.*

1 The fastest land animal is the tiger.

2 The spine-tailed swift flies faster than an eagle.

3 The black mamba can move at 11kph.

4 135kph is the same as 84mph.

5 Swordfish can swim at over 75kph.

6 A bee can fly at up to 32kph.

● Moving on ●

1 Which fact do you find most interesting? Explain why.

2 What do the following words mean?

  a) surging   **b**) pursuit   **c**) achieve

3 Name some other ways in which animals protect themselves.

4 Which of the animals opposite is the most fearsome? Say why.

i Use a dictionary if you need help.

STUDY SKILLS

● Getting information from charts ●

puppy's weight	amount of food per day
450g *(1 lb)*	50-75g *(2-3 oz)*
900g *(2 lb)*	75-100g *(3-4 oz)*
2.25kg *(5 lb)*	150-175g *(5-6 oz)*
4.5kg *(10 lb)*	275-350g *(10-12 oz)*
6.75kg *(15 lb)*	425g *(15 oz)*
9kg *(20 lb)*	550g *(20 oz)*
11.25kg *(25 lb)*	700g *(25 oz)*
18 kg *(40 lb)*	1 kg *(2¼ lb)*

i Abbreviations used:

oz = ounces

lb = pound (16 ounces)

g = gram

kg = kilogram

Use the chart above to help you answer these questions.

1 What is the lightest puppy weight shown in the chart?

2 What is the heaviest puppy weight shown?

3 What is 10 pound in kilograms?

4 What is 20 ounces in grams?

5 If you had a puppy which weighed 5 pounds how much food would it need each day?

6 If you gave your puppy 25 ounces of food every day, what weight would your puppy be?

extra

Choose one small and one large dog. Do some research and write some facts about each.

Small dogs: *Yorkshire Terrier, Chihuahua, Pekinese*

Large dogs: *Labrador, Great Dane, St Bernard*

11

WORD STUDY

● Words ending with 'ar', 'er' and 'or' ●

Decide whether ar, er *or* or *should go at the end of each word.*
Write the words in your book.

vicar

builder

doctor

1 caretak _ _   2 solicit _ _   3 direct _ _

4 pill _ _   5 begg _ _   6 bak _ _

7 radiat _ _   8 visit _ _   9 plumb _ _

10 cell _ _   11 sug _ _   12 dictat _ _

Draw a chart and group the words into sets like this:

'ar' words	**'er'** words	**'or'** words

● Words beginning with 'ex' ●

extend	excitement	exhausted	excellent
extreme	except	exhale	execute
	exceed	excess	

1 Write the two words that begin with 'ext'.
2 Write the two words that begin with 'exh'.
3 Write the one word that begins with 'exe'.
4 Write the five words that begin with 'exc'.

LANGUAGE STUDY

● Plurals ●

Copy into your book the rules about making singular nouns into plural nouns. For each rule add five more examples.

1 Most singular nouns become plural just by adding an 's'.
Example: dog → dogs

2 Most nouns ending in 'ch', 'sh', 'ss' or 'x' are changed into the plural by adding 'es'.
Example: church → churches

3 Most nouns ending in a 'consonant + y' change the 'y' to 'ies' in the plural.
Example: baby → babies

4 Most nouns ending in 'f' or 'fe' change to 'ves' in the plural.
Example: knife → knives.

5 Most nouns ending in a 'vowel + o' add 's' in the plural.
Example: radio → radios

6 Most nouns ending in a 'consonant + o' add 'es' in the plural.
Example: potato → potatoes

7 Some words do not follow any of these rules!
Example: foot → feet

More about nouns
● Concrete and abstract nouns ●

In your book draw a chart and divide these nouns into two sets according to whether they are concrete or abstract nouns.

height	love	banana	book	honesty
water	alligator	wonder	anger	
tree	television	patience	car	school
opinion	darkness	mouse		

concrete nouns	abstract nouns

Singular means one.

a lion cub

Plural means more than one.

lots of lion cubs

Concrete nouns are things you can touch, see, taste or smell. e.g. biscuit, sand, bird.

Abstract nouns are thoughts and ideas that can't be touched, seen etc. e.g. speed, height, love.

extra

Write down all the abstract nouns you can think of to do with feelings people sometimes have e.g. love, jealousy.

13

WRITING WORKSHOP

● Missing sentences ●

Write a sensible second sentence for each of these like this:

1 The lion roared loudly.
   It leapt to its feet and raced after the hunter.

2 The doctor opened her bag.
   _____

3 The sky grew dark.
   _____

4 An arrow whizzed through the air.
   _____

Now make up a first sentence for each of these.

5 _____ . Then we bought an ice cream.
6 _____ . We hurried to shelter under a tree.
7 _____ . Suddenly the screen went blank.
8 _____ . It made me feel quite scared.

● Silly sentences ●

Explain what is wrong with each of these sentences.

1 The game ended in a draw after Ben scored the winning goal.
2 Jo's twin sister is a year older than she is.
3 Most of the lies Yasmin told were true.
4 Aunt Emily gave birth to her baby tomorrow.

extra

Make up some silly sentences like these of your own.

● Punctuate the passage ●

Rewrite this passage in your book. Punctuate it correctly.

it was a dark moonless night in sherwood forest strange scratching noises were coming from behind the tree what could they be the air was hot damp and sticky ben broke out into a sweat as he approached his heart pounded loudly whoosh suddenly a startled bird rose up into the air ben laughed aloud as he realised what it was

i In this passage there should be:

11 capital letters
 2 commas
 7 full stops
  an exclamation mark
  a question mark

● Expressing opinions ●

People have different opinions on almost everything!

I believe it's cruel to keep lions in captivity. They should be allowed to be free, in their natural environment.

In the wild, lions get hunted and die of starvation. In a zoo they are well cared for and fed.

Think of several reasons to support each of these points of view.

Write them under two headings in your book.

a) All zoos should be closed.

b) Zoos do good things.

● Design a poster ●

Choose one of the views above to support. Design a poster to persuade people about your views.

Clear message

Bold picture

Catchy slogan

A few brief points

CLOSE ALL ZOOS

Would <u>YOO</u> live in a zoo?

* Zoos are not natural
*
*

extra

Consider what different views there could be on whether it is kind to keep animals as pets. Write down as many as you can.

15

Pandora's Box
(an old Greek myth)

In the beginning…

Prometheus created men and women and the god Zeus breathed life into the people he had made. Everything went well until one day Prometheus decided to play a trick on Zeus. This angered the god so much that he put out all fire on earth. People became very cold and hungry. Because Prometheus loved humans he stole a ray of sunshine to warm them. Zeus did not like anyone getting the better of him so he decided to punish Prometheus and all of mankind. He ordered the gods to create a beautiful woman named Pandora, and ordered Epimetheus to marry her.

The story continues like this…

Pandora was vain and self-centred.

She nagged her husband constantly.

She demanded he open a special locked box. Epimetheus refused,

as Prometheus had entrusted the box to his care.

In the box was trapped every known evil and disease.

But her husband's stubborness made Pandora more determined.

Convinced the box held jewels, she planned to steal it.

To be continued…

Retold by Marcia Williams

COMPREHENSION

● Starting points ●

Complete these sentences in your book.

1 In the Greek myth, Prometheus created …
2 Zeus got so angry he …
3 To make the humans warm, Prometheus …
4 Pandora was …
5 Pandora nagged her husband to …
6 In the box …

● Moving on ●

1 Write one example of kindness in the story.
2 Write one example of pride in the story.
3 Write one example of greed in the story.
4 Look up and write the definition of a 'myth'.
   Explain why you think this story is classed as a myth.

> A thesaurus is a book of words with similar meaning. It is set out rather like a dictionary.

STUDY SKILLS

● Using a thesaurus ●

Below is an extract from a typical thesaurus.

part of speech (verb)   synonyms (words with similar meaning)
key word   antonym (opposite meaning)

evaporate	*v.*	vanish, vaporise, disappear	*appear*
evening	*n.*	dusk, nightfall, twilight	*dawn*
ever	*adv.*	always, forever, evermore	*never*
evil	*adj.*	wicked, sinful, wrong	*good*
excuse	1. *n.*	plea, apology, reason	
	2. *v.*	free, forgive, exempt	

> **Abbreviations used**
> *adj.* = adjective
> *adv.* = adverb
> *n.* = noun
> *v.* = verb

1 Which of these words is a noun, verb, adjective, adverb?
   a) evening   **b**) evil   **c**) evaporate   **d**) ever
2 Write three words which mean the same as 'evil'.
3 Write three synonyms for 'evaporate'.
4 Which word means 'always'?
5 Which word can be used both as a noun and a verb?
6 'Dawn' is the opposite of which word?
7 What does 'antonym' mean?
8 Write another word for 'apology'.

> ## *extra*
> Use a thesaurus to find some synonyms for: necessary, nice, noise, normal, neat, naughty.

17

WORD STUDY

● Word beginnings ●

Look for the words beginning with 'con', 'en' and 'pro' that are hidden in the box.

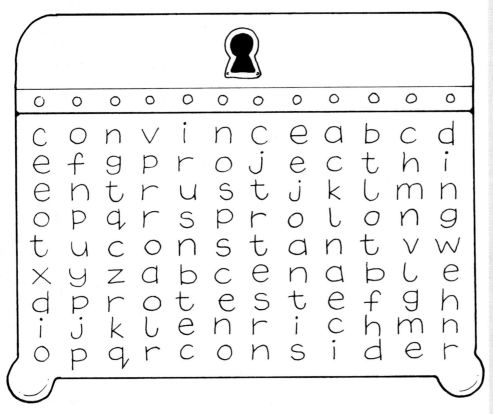

1 Find and write the three words beginning with 'con'.
2 Find and write the three words beginning with 'en'.
3 Find and write the three words beginning with 'pro'.
4 Choose six of the words. Write some sentences containing each word.

● Palindromes ●

Write all these words backwards in your book. What do you notice?

noon   deed   peep   civic   bob   toot   radar   rotator

Sometimes a sentence or a phrase can be a palindrome. Write which of these are palindromes.

1 My dog is hot.
3 What cat is that?
5 Madam, I'm Adam.
7 Niagara, O roar again!

2 Draw, O coward!
4 Sad? I'm Midas.
6 The frog on a log.
8 A man, a plan, a canal - Panama.

---

extra

Here are some prefixes which come from the Greek language:

tele- (means from afar)

mono- (means single)

auto- (means self)

dia- (means through)

Find some words which begin with each of these. Write them down.

i Prefixes are letters that are put at the beginning of words.

i A palindrome is a word, phrase or sentence that reads the same backwards or forwards.

18

LANGUAGE STUDY

● Parts of speech ●

There are several different types of words in English called 'Parts of Speech'. I have collected some of these and put them into boxes for you.

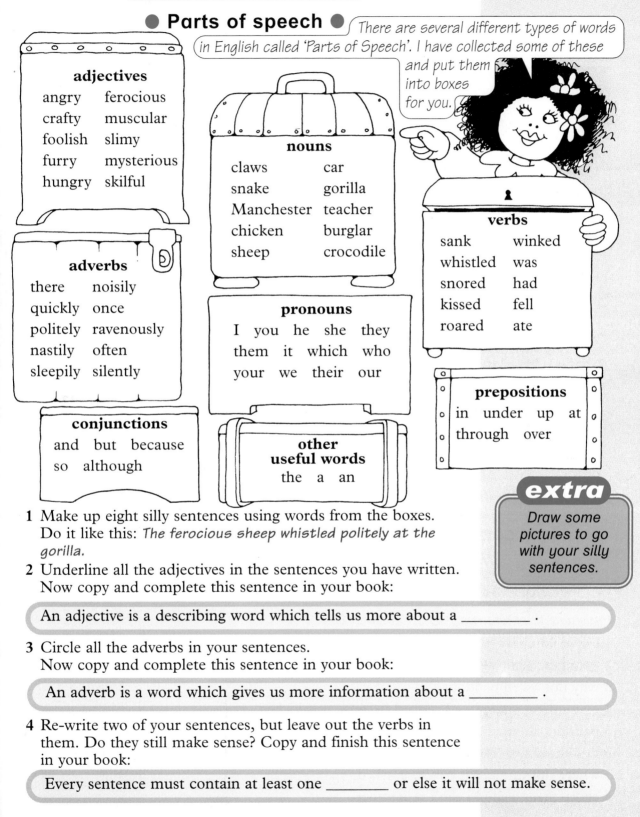

adjectives

angry   ferocious
crafty   muscular
foolish   slimy
furry   mysterious
hungry   skilful

nouns

claws   car
snake   gorilla
Manchester   teacher
chicken   burglar
sheep   crocodile

verbs

sank   winked
whistled   was
snored   had
kissed   fell
roared   ate

adverbs

there   noisily
quickly   once
politely   ravenously
nastily   often
sleepily   silently

pronouns

I   you   he   she   they
them   it   which   who
your   we   their   our

prepositions

in   under   up   at
through   over

conjunctions

and   but   because
so   although

other useful words

the   a   an

1 Make up eight silly sentences using words from the boxes.
   Do it like this: *The ferocious sheep whistled politely at the gorilla.*

2 Underline all the adjectives in the sentences you have written.
   Now copy and complete this sentence in your book:

   An adjective is a describing word which tells us more about a _____ .

3 Circle all the adverbs in your sentences.
   Now copy and complete this sentence in your book:

   An adverb is a word which gives us more information about a _____ .

4 Re-write two of your sentences, but leave out the verbs in them. Do they still make sense? Copy and finish this sentence in your book:

   Every sentence must contain at least one _____ or else it will not make sense.

extra

Draw some pictures to go with your silly sentences.

19

WRITING WORKSHOP

● Direct speech ●

Let me have a look inside that box.

I'm sorry. I promised I wouldn't open it.

Go on! One little look won't hurt.

No. I will not break my word.

Copy these sentences.
Complete the words inside the speech marks.

"   Let me have a look inside that box   ," Pandora asked.

"_____," Epimetheus replied.

"_____," Pandora whined.

"_____," Epimetheus said sternly.

Whenever someone different speaks always start a new line.

ⓘ In writing, when people speak directly to each other we use **speech marks** (or **inverted commas**).

Whatever you would put in speech bubbles goes <u>inside</u> the speech marks.

● Two common patterns of dialogue ●

Pattern 1: Sam said, "I'm going to call for my friend."

Pattern 2: "I'm going to call for my friend," said Sam.

Punctuate these sentences correctly in your book.

1 i'll let you have a sweet if you open the box said pandora

2 epimetheus answered i can't open the box

3 why not asked pandora

4 epimetheus smiled and replied because it is locked

5 pandora shouted well give me the key then

6 i'm afraid i've lost it epimetheus said quietly

7 where did you lose it pandora asked

8 epimetheus sighed i can't remember

ⓘ **Dialogue** means just the words people say.

extra

Make up and write a conversation between a child and a mum. The boy or girl is trying to persuade the grown-up they need a new bike.

● Pandora's Box - continued ●

Write which of these words you could use to describe Pandora.

spoilt   lovely

thoughtful   crafty

generous   devious

nagging   kind

nasty   dishonest

loving   scheming

The beginning and middle of my story is on page 16. Read it again carefully, then read how it continues.

One day, while
Epimetheus slept,

Pandora gets what Pandora wants.

Pandora stole the
box and its key.

I can't wait to see what treasures you contain.

Eagerly, she fitted
the key into the lock.

And now to lift the lid…

It turned, and she
lifted the lid…

How do you think the story ended? These questions should help you.

What happened when Pandora
opened the lid?

What did she find in the box?

What happened to Pandora?

How did Epimetheus react?

Was Zeus happy with the trick
he'd played?

extra

Write out your strip cartoon as a story using speech marks.

• *Write your ideas in rough first.*
• *Choose your best ideas.*
• *Present them in the form of a strip cartoon.*
• *Use speech bubbles for the characters.*
• *Put a simple caption (sentence) underneath each picture.*

Biting air
Winds blow
City streets
Under snow

Noses red
Lips sore
Runny eyes
Hands raw

Chimneys smoke
Cars crawl
Piled snow
On garden wall

Slush in gutters
Ice in lanes
Frosty patterns
On window panes

Morning call
Lift up your head
Nipped by winter
Stay in bed.

Gareth Owen

COMPREHENSION

● Starting points ●

Read the poem and write what the poet says...

1 ...are under snow.   **2** ...are red.

3 ... are raw.   **4** ... crawl.

5 ... is in gutters.   **6** ... is on window panes.

extra

Find some other 'wintry' poems. Choose one you really like. Make a copy of it in your best writing and illustrate it.

● Moving on ●

1 The poet makes winter days sound very unpleasant. Write three things he says which make you feel very cold when you read them.

2 Now write several things about snow that you enjoy.

3 What do you think the poet means by

  a) biting air?   **b**) cars crawl?

4 Read the last verse again. Write how you feel on a cold winter's morning and how hard it is to get out of your lovely warm bed.

STUDY SKILLS

Flow diagram
● *Making a bird table* ●

You will need:

Think carefully how you would make this bird table.
Write your instructions in the form of a flow diagram like this:

> You will need...
>
> First of all you must...
>
> Next you...

extra

Draw a flow diagram giving the instructions for making a snowman.

i Write your ideas in rough first. Read them carefully and check you haven't missed anything before you draw your flow diagram.

WORD STUDY

● Syllables ●

Work out these 'ment' words and write them in your book.
They each have three syllables.

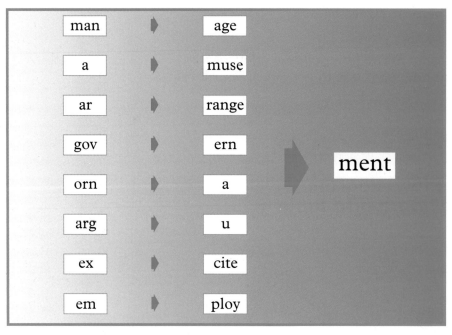

man	▶	age
a	▶	muse
ar	▶	range
gov	▶	ern
orn	▶	a
arg	▶	u
ex	▶	cite
em	▶	ploy

ment

Which word ….

1 means being excited?

2 has the word 'range' in it?

3 makes you smile?

4 is about having a row?

5 is something you use for decoration?

6 has the word 'age' in it?

7 is to do with being in charge?

8 means a job?

● Homophones ●

Write two sentences for each pair of words to show you understand
their meaning.

1 tale tail   2 saw sore

3 steel steal   4 past passed

5 aloud allowed   6 grown groan

7 poor pour   8 piece peace

---

i If you say a word slowly you can break it down into smaller parts. These are called **syllables**. Each syllable must have at least one vowel or 'y' in it.

extra

Write some more words ending with the suffix 'ment'. Work out how many syllables there are in each of the words you write.

i **Homophones** are words that sound alike but have different meanings.

LANGUAGE STUDY

● Adverbs of manner ●

I ran *quickly*.

I dropped the drum *noisily*.

I stroked the cat *gently*.

Change these sets of adjectives into adverbs of manner *in your book.*

SET 1
a) clever *cleverly*   b) sweet   c) sudden
d) poor   e) willing   f) anxious

SET 2
a) hungry *hungrily*   b) angry   c) lucky
d) noisy   e) easy   f) lazy

SET 3
a) simple *simply*   b) gentle   c) horrible
d) miserable   e) noble   f) comfortable

SET 4
a) hopeful *hopefully*   b) careful   c) loyal
d) accidental   e) truthful   f) equal

● Adverbs of time ●

Make up some sentences and use these adverbs of time *in them.*

> soon   now   before   already   then

● Adverbs of place ●

Make up some sentences and use these adverbs of place *in them.*

> here   there   everywhere   nowhere

i An **adverb** tells you more about a verb. **An adverb of manner** tells you *how* something happened.

extra

Explain the rule you use for changing each set like this:
Rule for Set 1
You just add the suffix 'ly' to the end of each adjective.

extra

Choose two adverbs from each set. Write sentences containing each adverb.

i An **adverb of time** tells you *when* something happened.

i An **adverb of place** tells you *where* something happened.

25

WRITING WORKSHOP

● Divided direct speech ●

*That's a funny joke.
I must remember to tell
that to my mum.*

One common pattern for writing dialogue is:

"That's a funny joke," chuckled Ben.
"I must remember to
 tell that to my mum."

Copy these sentences.
Use the pattern above to punctuate these sentences.

1 stay exactly where you are shouted the gunman dont move or ill shoot

2 start digging here ordered peg leg jake this is where the treasure is buried

3 close that door dad cried its cold with it open

4 ive been chosen as captain joanne boasted that will show them who is the best

5 this is my final offer the car salesman said do you want it or not

6 my grandad is getting very old sam said hes seventy five tomorrow

● Dialogue in playlet form ●

Shiraz: I'm freezing! That wind is like a knife!
Raza: It's beginning to get too dark to carry on. I think we'll have to stop for the night.
Shiraz: I don't like the look of the sky either. It looks like more snow.
Raza: We need to find a sheltered spot, somewhere out of the wind.
Shiraz: How about that cave over there? That looks a possibility.
Raza: Come on then. Let's go and have a closer look.

Write out the conversation above in your book. Set it out using speech marks like this:

Shiraz shivered and said, "I'm freezing! That wind is like a knife."

extra

Develop this conversation:

1 Continue it as a play. Introduce some other characters and a narrator.

2 Make it into a story. Use more dialogue (people saying things) in your story. Think of an unexpected ending.

● Writing a poem ●

Read the poem on page 22 again. Here's the first verse to think about.

Biting air
Winds blow
City streets
Under snow

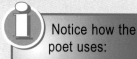

Notice how the poet uses:
● four **lines** in each **verse**
● short phrases
● interesting words

Follow the pattern of Winter Days.
Use this pattern to make up your own poem called Summer Days.
Give it three verses. Give each verse a different theme:

> Verse 1 - the weather
>
> Verse 2 - what you see
>
> Verse 3 - how it makes you feel.

Write down lots of ideas for each verse in rough first. ~~birds' song~~

bathed in sun ~~meadow grass~~
~~sunset glow~~ seaside ~~hot sun~~
cool breeze bees' buzzing farmers' fields
countryside
warm air

Choose the ideas you like best.
Check for silly spelling mistakes.
Arrange them in order.
(They don't have to rhyme.)

Here are my ideas for the first verse.

Warm air
Cool breeze
countryside
Bathed in sun

Hot sun

Where will you put illustrations?

Will you word process your poem or write it in your best handwriting?

Will you print the title and decorate it?

Will you have a decorated border?

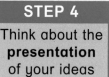

STEP 1
Make a **plan**

STEP 2
Draft your ideas

STEP 3
Revise and **edit** your ideas

STEP 4
Think about the **presentation** of your ideas

Now write and present your finished poem.

The Only Survivors!

THE SUN had only been up an hour or so. It was already uncomfortably hot.

The tree gave some shade but not much. The ground was scorched and dry, except for a small trickle of water which was an apology for a stream. Its water was muddy and thick - but at least it was cool! Along the side of the gully in which the water ran were a few other bushes and spindly trees, but not much seemed to grow on the huge flat plain that stretched out in front of them. There were a few clumps of bushes and some enormous rocks scattered around but not a lot of shelter or cover.

Jamie sat silently with his back against the tree, staring at the mangled, burnt-out wreckage of the aircraft. The horror of the crash, the noise, the flames, the panic was all he could think about. Joanne knew she had to do something. She made her decision. She wasn't to know that it was a bad one. 'It's no good staying around here,' she said grimly. She stood up. With a determined expression on her face she pulled Jamie up and pointed. 'We must head for those hills,' she said bravely.

In the distance, in the haze, wooded hills rose into the sky. The gully, with its pathetic little stream, ran down towards the plain. They looked desperately for some sign of hope. They could see no roads, no houses, no people, nothing moving at all. It looked completely uninhabited. It looked terrifying.

COMPREHENSION

● Starting points ●

In your book, write what you think the missing words should be.

The sun had only been up for a short _____(1)_____ , but it was already _____(2)_____ hot. Joanne and _____(3)_____ were sitting under a _____(4)_____ near a small _____(5)_____ .

The children had been in an _____(6)_____ that had crashed.

The aircraft had crashed on a huge, flat _____(7)_____ . There were no roads, no houses and no _____(8)_____ to be seen.

Joanne decided they had to do _____(9)_____ . She decided they should _____(10)_____ for the hills in the distance.

● Moving on ●

1 Where do you think the children were going in the aircraft?

2 How many people survived the crash? How do you know?

3 What sort of girl do you think Joanne was?

4 Why do you think it says that Joanne's decision was a bad one? Do you think it would have been better to stay near the aircraft?

STUDY SKILLS

● Justifying choices ●

Which five of the following things would you choose to have to help you survive? Give a reason for choosing each item. Write your answers in your book. List your five choices in order of importance.

WORD STUDY

● Jumbled letters ●

Work out what these anagrams are. All the words appear in the story. Write them out correctly. Use the meanings to help you.

1 samfle   These are hot. You find them in a fire.

2 eewragck   What was left after the crash.

3 yaplogo   This is what you give when you are sorry.

4 plmuc   A group of trees or bushes.

5 sidonice   You make this when you decide.

6 smarte   This is like a small river.

An anagram is a word which has had its letters jumbled up in a different order to make a different word e.g. *tar* is an anagram for *rat*.

extra

Make up some anagrams of different types of transport.

● Suffixing verbs ●

Copy and complete this table in your book:

Verb	+ ing	+ ed
quarrel	quarrelling	quarrelled
permit	_____	permitted
regret	regretting	_____
occur	_____	occurred
_____	preferring	_____
_____	_____	recurred
travel	_____	_____
signal	signalling	_____
_____	fulfilling	_____
_____	_____	controlled

In words of more than one syllable, if the last syllable has only one vowel you must double the last consonant before adding a suffix beginning with a vowel.

LANGUAGE STUDY

● Verb tenses ●

Re-write the sentences and change the verbs from the past tense into the future tense.
The first sentence has been done for you.

1 a) James <u>sat</u> quietly.
  James <u>will sit</u> quietly.

  b) Joanne <u>spoke</u> bravely to James.

  c) The band <u>played</u> in the park.

  d) The woman <u>gave</u> the old clothes to the beggar.

  e) The monkeys <u>swung</u> from the branches.

  f) The children <u>walked</u> home in the rain.

Now rewrite each sentence in the present tense in two different ways like this:

2 a) James is sitting quietly.   James sits quietly.

i a) Verbs in the **past tense** means the action took place some time ago e.g. *Yesterday it rained.*

b) Verbs in the **future tense** means the action will take place some time in the future e.g. *It will rain tomorrow.*

c) Verbs in the **present tense** means they are happening now. e.g. *It is raining now.*

● Collective nouns ●

a clump of bushes   a flock of sheep

In your book complete these collective nouns by using words from the box.

1 a _____ of fish

2 a _____ of bananas

3 a _____ of cows

4 a _____ of ships

5 a _____ of spectators

6 a _____ of wolves

7 a _____ of whales

8 a _____ of sticks

fleet
crowd
shoal
pack
bundle
school
bunch
herd

31

WRITING WORKSHOP

● A TV interview ●

Imagine you were being interviewed for TV about something exciting you have done. It can be true or you can make it up.

*Write the **script** of your **report**. Set it out like this:*

REPORTER: Good evening. Tonight I'm interviewing someone with a very exciting story. Would you like to tell the viewers all about it?

YOU: Well, it all started in the middle of the night.
(Write your name)

REPORTER: What happened then?

● Writing a description ●

Read the opening paragraph of the story on page 28 again. Notice how many adjectives the author uses to make it more interesting.

- Imagine you have crashed onto the side of a high, snow-covered mountain at night.

- Write a paragraph giving a vivid description of the landscape.

- Put in a lot of detail. Use some interesting adjectives to help you.

- Make your paragraph into the beginning of an adventure story.

- Use the story plan to help you.

extra

Here is an outline of the **story plan** to go with the description you have written.

- head for hills
- problems of cold and no food
- find cave
- wolves attack
- slip and hurt foot
- hear helicopter
- try to attract attention
- rescue

● Writing a newspaper report ●

MYSTERY PLANE CRASH TWO SURVIVE TO TELL ALL!

Miracles do happen!
It was thought no one could survive such a crash - but two plucky children did, and live to tell the tale.

Joanne and her brother Jamie were picked up by a search and rescue plane earlier today.

It had been sent out after flight MUN 412 had mysteriously crashed into an uninhabited area of desert. The children were tired, dirty and stunned. 'It's been terrible,' Joanne said, clutching her brother's hand tightly. 'It all started when…

Newspaper reports often have:

◀ a catchy headline

a photograph

mainly factual information.

(Note the importance of the opening sentence. It must get the reader's attention!)

They told me some of their most exciting adventures. I also asked them what they are planning to do now.

- Imagine you are a newspaper reporter.
- You meet Joanne and Jamie.
- Write a short report on their story.
- Set it out like the front page of the newspaper above.

extra

Choose one of these and write the story behind the headline.

GRANNY GRABS GANGSTER

ELEPHANT IN BURGER BAR

DUKE disappears

Do you remember?

STUDY SKILLS

> These sentences, explaining how to use a dictionary, are in the wrong order. Re-write them correctly and set them out like a flow diagram.

Use the guidewords at the top of each page to find the exact page you want.

You decide to look it up in a dictionary.

Carefully scan down the words on the page, using your knowledge of alphabetical order, until you find the word you want.

You decide what letter (or letters) the word starts with.

You come across a word you don't know or are not sure how to spell.

Open the dictionary to the section with the letter your word begins with.

WORD STUDY

doctor exciting protest occurring burglar
signalled contestant encourage musical builder

Use the words in the box. Write a word:

a) with the prefix 'en' **b)** ending in 'or'
c) with the suffix 'ed' **d)** ending in 'er'
e) with three syllables **f)** with 'al' at the end
g) starting with 'ex' **h)** with the suffix 'ing'
i) ending with 'ar' **j)** starting with 'con'

LANGUAGE STUDY

1 *Use these words to make up a sentence.*
(You will need to use 'the' three times.)

adjective	adverb	verb	preposition	nouns	definite article
frightened	angrily	chased	across	bull, boy, field	the

2 *Change these adjectives into adverbs of manner ending in 'ly'*

a) glad   **b**) nervous   **c**) easy   **d**) lazy

e) ample   **f**) terrible   **g**) musical   **h**) joyful

3 *Write the singular of these plurals.*

a) girls   **b**) foxes   **c**) brushes   **d**) glasses

e) cities   **f**) supplies   **g**) wives   **h**) thieves

i) tomatoes   **j**) videos   **k**) fish   **l**) men

WRITING WORKSHOP

1 *Write out what each person said in the picture.*
Use speech marks.

Why are you late?

I got chased by a bull!

2 *Copy these sentences. Punctuate them correctly.*

Whats the time Tom asked

Tess replied Im not sure I think its nearly lunch time

My stomachs rumbling so I know you must be right Tom said

Youre always hungry Tess said with a smile You must have hollow legs

35

Animal names

1 ANIMAL NAMES FROM GREEK

Did you know that the hippopotamus got its name from the Greek word for river horse? *Hippos* means horse and *potamus* means river. Rhinoceros is a Latin word but it also came from the Greek language. Its name describes the main features of the animal - *rinos* means nose and *keras* means a horn. Rhinoceros therefore literally means 'nose with a horn'!

2

In Latin *leopardus* is the name for the leopard, *leon* is the name for lion and *camelos* is the name for camel. A porcupine's name has rather an interesting background. It comes from two Latin words, *porcus* meaning a swine, and *spina* meaning a thorn. So a porcupine is 'a pig with thorns'.

3

The Anglo-Saxon word *belkan* meant to roar. It is from this word that we have got the word bull. *Doer* in Anglo-Saxon meant a wild animal but it has now come to be the name for a deer, which is hardly a ferocious wild animal! Wolf is the modern spelling of the Anglo-Saxon word *wulf*. The Anglo-Saxon name for fox is *fax* (which actually means hair-mane). Dog is derived from another Anglo-Saxon (or Old English) name too. The word for dog in Anglo-Saxon is *doega*.

4

In Egypt cats were called *pasht*, which actually meant the moon, because that's when cats went out and about. This was shortened to *pas*, from which we get the name puss.

COMPREHENSION

● Starting points ●

1 Which animal's name really means:
  a) river horse?   **b)** nose with a horn?   **c)** hair mane?
  d) pig with thorns?   **e)** the moon?

2 Which animal gets its name from a word meaning 'to roar'?

● Moving on ●

1 Use a dictionary to find out the meaning of these words:

    a) derived   **b**) originate   **c**) etymology

2 The passage shows how we use language for naming things. Make a list of all the ways you can think of that we use spoken language, e.g. to explain, to instruct, etc.

3 Think of some other animals with unusual names, e.g. dragon fly, humming bird. Make up some reasons how these animals might have got their names. (They don't have to be true!)

4 Make up some animal names of your own. (See the *DIY animal names* box for some ideas.)

> **DIY animal names**
> You can:
>
> • take parts of the names of two animals and make one of them e.g. a lion and tiger becomes a liger.
>
> • think of a name of an animal and change it slightly. e.g. a snake becomes a snyke.

STUDY SKILLS

● Page layout - *sub-headings* ●

Read paragraphs 2, 3 and 4 on page 36 again. Think of suitable sub-headings for each paragraph. Write them in your book.

Pets in the home

• *Make up and write some information called 'Pets in the home'.*

• *Set out your writing in separate paragraphs.*

• *Write a paragraph under each of the following sub-headings:*

    - **Why people keep pets**

    - **Cats**

    - **Dogs**

    - **Rabbits**

> The whole passage on page 36 is called 'Animal names'. Each paragraph has its own sub-heading, according to the main idea of the paragraph. The first paragraph is all about animal names we get from the Greek language.

• *Add a final paragraph of your own. Make up your own sub-heading for it.*

WORD STUDY

● Roman words ●

In your book match up the English words in the Word Box that you think come from these Roman words.

 Many of the words we use today have come from other languages in the past.

Roman words	English words
STRATA	*street*
PORTUS	gate
MILLUS PASSUS	mile
VINUM	wine
CASTRA	camp
VALLUM	wall
CAESUS	cheese

Word Box

wine
cheese
wall
street
mile
camp
port

● Anglo-Saxon (Old English) words ●

In your book, write what you think each of these words meant.

Family words	Food or drink	Animals	Colours
moder	milc	hors	silfer
faeder	buture	doega	hwit
sunu	fisc	pigga	grene
dohter	mete	mus	brun

 When the Angles and Saxons invaded they brought many words into our language.

38

LANGUAGE STUDY

● Our language has changed ●

Write in modern English what you think is being said in the picture.

> What hast thou in thy goblet? It runneth over.

> Sire, I bring thee wine to quaff.

Now read this description of a man written by the famous English writer Chaucer in the 15th century.

Syngynge he was, or flotynge al the daye. He was as fresshe as the month of May. Short was hys gowne, with sleves longe and wyde. Wel koude he sit on hors, and faire ryde.

Here is the first sentence in modern English. Write what you think the other sentences say.

He was singing or whistling all day.

● New words ●

Copy this list of words into your book. Underline those which you think have entered our language in the last hundred years.

1 video   2 farmer
3 television   4 computer
5 car   6 astronaut
7 fog   8 refrigerator
9 radio   10 pizza

> Can you think of any other new words that may have been added to our language this century? Write them in your book.

> Our language is changing all the time. We are always changing words or adding new words to it.

39

WRITING WORKSHOP

● Using commas in lists ●

1 *Write two sentences about these pictures.*

   a) In the bowl there are …   **b)** On the table there is …

2 *Now copy and punctuate these sentences with commas.*

   a) In the window there was a doll a football a bike a torch a jigsaw and a magic kit.

   b) I enjoy maths science history art and games.

   c) Out of my window I saw a man pulling a sledge some children playing snowballs an old lady going shopping and a dog rolling in the snow.

Using commas to separate
● people's names, or after 'yes' or 'no' ●

Copy this conversation and put in the missing commas.

Teacher: Jo why is your writing untidy?

Jo: Our dog kept jumping on me.

Teacher: Do you think that's a good excuse Jo?

Jo: No Mrs Hunt.

Teacher: Well Jo I think you had better do it again.

Jo: Yes Mrs Hunt.

Using commas in
● long sentences to separate phrases ●

Copy and punctuate these sentences with commas. Put them where you think a pause sounds right. Do it like this:

1 The brave boy, who had broken his leg, still managed to smile.

2 The tiger which was sleeping woke up when the impala leapt past.

3 The icy wind which blew all night froze the lake.

4 The chef who had won many prizes for cooking made a great cake.

5 Mrs Smith our next door neighbour has been very ill.

6 The pyramids which are in Egypt are very old.

7 Tom my little brother can be a bit of a nuisance at times.

8 Ben Nevis the highest mountain in Scotland can get very cold.

We use commas to show the reader where to pause.

The most common uses of commas are:

• to separate items in a list

• to separate names of people, or after 'yes' or 'no'

• in long sentences to make a short pause when extra phrases are put in.

● Writing an information leaflet ●

The problem: What information about your school would you give to a family thinking of moving to your area?

The task: To produce a basic information leaflet about the school.

What will you put in your leaflet?

You might include:

- a photo or drawing of the school
- a brief history of the school
- what classes and staff are in the school
- the curriculum (the subjects you learn)
- a list of after school clubs and activities
- details of your uniform
- anything else you think is important.

A ten-point action plan:

1 Decide what sections you are going to include.

2 Produce each section (along with drawings, maps, plans, illustrations etc.) in your own writing or on a computer. Do each on a separate piece of paper. Give each section a clear heading.

3 Read through each section carefully. Change anything you don't like. Add anything you have missed out.

4 Check that each section:
   - makes sense
   - contains no spelling mistakes
   - is punctuated correctly.

5 Cut out each finished section.

6 Arrange your sections in their final order.

7 Arrange the sections onto sheets of paper. Think about how you want each page to look. Consider where you want your illustrations and pictures. Make sure you have space!

8 Stick the sections onto paper and finish off the final artwork.

9 Decide if you need a contents page or you wish to number each page.

10 Design an eye-catching front and back cover. Ensure the title is clear and attractively printed. Finally, staple your leaflet together.

When you give information try to keep it brief and to the point. Set it out clearly. Look at page 36 to get some ideas.

extra

*Make up a **Code of Conduct** for welcoming new pupils. Start like this:*

1 Before the pupil arrives ask your teacher for some information about him or her.

2 When they arrive, make sure that you give them a warm welcome ...

The House on the Hill

If you visit the House on the Hill for a dare
remember my words … 'There are dangers. Beware!'

> The piano's white teeth,
> when you plonk out a note,
> will bite off your fingers then reach for your throat.
> The living room curtains
> – long, heavy and black –
> will wrap you in cobwebs
> if you're slow to step back.

When you enter the House on the Hill for a dare
remember my words … 'There are dangers. Beware!'

> The fridge in the kitchen
> has a self-closing door.
> If it locks you inside then you're ice cubes for sure.
> The steps to the cellar
> are littered with bones,
> and up from the darkness
> drift creakings and groans.

If you go to the House on the Hill for a dare
remember my words … 'There are dangers. Beware!'   *Wes Magee*

COMPREHENSION

● Starting points ●

Choose the best ending for each sentence.

1 The piano's white teeth will

  a) bite your nails. **b)** bite off your fingers. **c)** grab your hands.

2 The living room curtains are
  a) long and grey. **b)** long, heavy and black. **c)** light and long.

3 You must step back quickly from the
  a) fridge. **b)** cellar door. **c)** curtains.

4 The curtains will wrap you in
  a) brown paper. **b)** ribbons. **c)** cobwebs.

5 The fridge will turn you into
  a) ice cubes. **b)** an ice lolly. **c)** ice cream.

6 The steps to the cellar are littered with
  a) rubbish. **b)** bones. **c)** litter.

● Moving on ●

1 Write some things you like (or don't like) about the poem.

2 Why do you think the poet repeats the same chorus three times (at the beginning, middle and end of the poem)?.

3 Describe what you think the house looks like from the outside.

4 What might you find in the cellar? Explain your answer.

STUDY SKILLS

In libraries, fiction books are arranged in alphabetical order according to the author's surname.

Organising fiction books - ● *alphabetical order* ●

Arrange these authors in alphabetical order according to their surnames.

Paula Danziger	Lucy Daniels	Annie Dalton
Andrew Davies	Roald Dahl	Colin Dann

● The author catalogue ●

This is a school's author catalogue. You would look for books by Roald Dahl in drawer (2).

Which drawers would you look in for books by these authors?

a) Philippa Pearce   **b**) Rose Impey   **c**) Barbara Mitchelhill

d) Geraldine Kay   **e**) Sheila Cavelle   **f**) Terry Pratchett

g) C.S. Lewis   **h**) Helen Cresswell   **i**) Margaret Mahy

i The way to find out if the library has the fiction book you want is to look in the **author catalogue**. This is often like a small chest of drawers which contains a card for every book in the library. The cards are stored in **alphabetical order**, just like the books.

extra

Choose five of the authors opposite. Use an author catalogue to find the title of one book each has written.

43

WORD STUDY

● Silent letters ●

Shhhh!

Shhhh!

The words below all contain either a silent 'c', 't', or 'u'. Draw a chart in your book and put the words in groups according to their silent letter. There will be four words in each group.

| guard | castle | muscle | guitar | science | scissors |
| build | listen | whistle | biscuit | scene | thistle |

silent 'c'	silent 't'	silent 'u'
mus*c*le	cas*t*le	g*u*ard

● Ghosts or phantoms? ●

Copy these words into your book. Decide whether the missing letters should be 'gh' or 'ph'.

1 ☐antom   **2** ☐ost   **3** tele☐one

4 ne☐ew   **5** tou☐   **6** wei☐t

7 ele☐ant   **8** fri☐t   **9** lau☐

10 ni☐t   **11** al☐abet   **12** ☐otogra☐

LANGUAGE STUDY

● Matching subjects and verbs ●

A ghost <u>likes</u> to play tricks
(singular)

Ghosts <u>like</u> to sing.
(plural)

1 *Think of suitable subjects for each sentence.*

a) A _____ lives in a haunted house.

b) _____ make webs to catch flies.

c) The wizard's _____ were long and bony.

d) _____ flew out of the bell tower towards me.

2 *Rewrite these sentences correctly.*

a) Sam and Ben was scared.

b) They doesn't like visiting the old house.

c) A ghost shriek and moan.

d) One of the boys are frightened.

> **i** Every sentence must have a **subject** and a **verb**. The subject in each sentence should *match* the verb. Singular nouns need singular verbs.
>
> Plural nouns need plural verbs.

● Subjects, verbs and objects ●

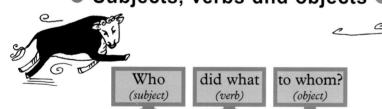

Who	did what	to whom?
(subject)	*(verb)*	*(object)*

The bull   chased   the girl.

Copy this chart and fill in each sentence with a subject and an object.

Subject	Verb	Object
	read	
	kissed	
	opened	
	attacked	
	scratched	
	tickled	
	cooked	
	ate	
	hated	

> **i** Most sentences have a **subject**, **verb** and an **object**.

> **extra**
>
> *Rewrite your sentences and make them more interesting by adding adjectives and adverbs. Do it like this:*
>
> *The huge bull angrily chased the screaming girl.*

45

WRITING WORKSHOP

● **Make it longer!** ●

Pattern for a poem

Start with a noun	The ghost
Add an adjective	The wailing ghost
Add another	The wailing, moaning ghost
Add a verb	The wailing, moaning ghost rose
Add an adverb	The wailing, moaning ghost rose hauntingly
Add an ending	The wailing, moaning ghost rose hauntingly from the hole in the floorboards
Add an adjective to the ending	The wailing, moaning ghost rose hauntingly from the gaping hole in the floorboards

Choose any noun you like.
Follow the pattern to make your own poem.

● **Make it shorter!** ●

This notice is too long. No one will read it!

This is better. It still has the same meaning but is much shorter!

Here is another notice that is too long. In your book make a shorter notice with the same meaning.

If you use the chains for rattling and scaring people would you please be kind enough to put them tidily back in the trunk when you have finished with them so other ghosts can use them. Thank you very much.

Please return the chains to the trunk when you've finished with them. Thanks

Visitors are kindly requested to sign their names in the Visitors Book and report to the main office as soon as they enter the school premises.

● Personality profile ●

My name is Shireen. I'm tall for my age with short, spiky hair and am a pretty smart dresser. My friends call me Sheen because I'm brilliant!

I love sport and am good at swimming and gymnastics. In fact there aren't many sports I don't enjoy. I'm a bundle of energy really, always willing to have a go at anything. Spiders, snakes, ghosts - nothing scares me!

My hobbies are music, art and standing on my head. I do have a habit of blinking but this means I don't see things that might worry me.

When you want to impress someone you want to get them to think of you in the best possible way. We can influence people by the way we write. Look how I wrote about myself.

• Write a personality profile of yourself.
• Make sure you mention all your good points.
• Try to make it fun, and make yourself sound interesting.

extra

Try writing a personality profile for someone else you know well.

● Feelings ●

frightened   excited   brave   curious

Think of a time when you felt each of these feelings. For each feeling write:

Characters: Were any other people involved?
Setting: When did it occur?
             Where were you?
             What was the situation that made you feel this way?
Action: What happened?
             What did people do and say?

extra

Feeling green with envy? Write what colours you associate with these feelings:

a) fear
b) sorrow
c) anger
d) jealousy
e) happiness

Albert Blows a Fuse

IT WAS rather tricky getting the television home. And it was even trickier making it work. It was worth all the trouble, though, because when the TV eventually burst into life it was wonderful! The soaps! The sport! The films! The advertisements! The advertisements? They were as good as the shows if not better. Albert realised that there was a whole world out there absolutely bursting with things to buy. There was no time to lose!

Albert began to realise that he was missing a lot of good entertainment on the other channels - so he bought a video. But he still had to leave the television to prepare his meals. So he got a microwave. He also moved his fridge and bed into the new TV room so he would never have to move - except to go to the loo, of course.

Soon, Albert had no money: this was not surprising because he had spent it all at 'Noyze'. He decided to sell his beautiful garden to Mr and Mrs Green next door. But he didn't mind - he could now buy more things. He particularly wanted a satellite dish. 'Wonderful, this technology,' Albert muttered to himself as he phoned 'Noyze' to order four new televisions, an extra video machine and a satellite dish or two.

Albert stacked up all his new equipment in his TV room. He could watch thirty different pictures at the same time. It was a bit noisy, and the television sets did stop the sun coming in. Albert didn't care though - he could see the pictures better without any sun. 'Boring old sun! Boring old people! Boring old world!' said Albert, switching channels on his remote control.

Tom Bower

COMPREHENSION

● Starting points ●

Write out these sentences again in the correct order.

- Then Albert got a microwave so he wouldn't have to prepare meals.
- He sold his garden to get more money.
- Albert bought his first TV set.
- Lastly he bought four more TVs, another video and a satellite dish.
- After this, Albert moved his bed and fridge into his TV room.
- Next he bought a video to record other programmes.

> Many stories have a message for the reader. They are making a special point. This is called the moral.

● Moving on ●

1 In your own words, describe the sort of person Albert was.
2 Write a list of what you think are the good and bad things about TV.
3 There are two references to 'Noyze' in the story. What do you think it is? Give reasons for your answer.
4 What do you think is the moral of the story?

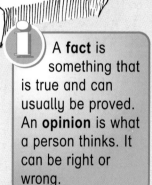

STUDY SKILLS

● Fact or opinion? ●

Write whether each of these statements is fact or opinion.
Give a reason for each choice.

1 Television is the best form of entertainment you can get.
2 The design of televisions is improving all the time.
3 Because of modern technology it is possible to receive TV pictures from all over the world.
4 On TV you can watch many different sorts of programmes.
5 News programmes are the most important.
6 Adverts are the most enjoyable thing on TV.
7 Adverts are usually made to persuade people to buy things.
8 In 1926 John Logie Baird showed it was possible to transmit visual images.
9 John Logie Baird was the cleverest inventor of all time.
10 John Logie Baird is known as the 'father of television'.

> **i** A **fact** is something that is true and can usually be proved. An **opinion** is what a person thinks. It can be right or wrong.

WORD STUDY

● Words containing 'ia', 'ie' and 'io' ●

Copy these words and choose either 'ia', 'ie' or 'io' to complete them.

1 rad __ __

2 rad __ __ tor

3 brill __ __ nt

4 barr __ __ r

5 aud __ __ nce

6 mill __ __ n

7 offic __ __ l

8 al __ __ n

9 stud __ __

10 opin __ __ n

11 immed __ __ te

12 exper __ __ nce

ℹ️ Use a dictionary to check if you are not sure of any words.

extra

Write some sentences and use each of the words.

● Deliberately spelling words incorrectly ●

Write what these should really say if they were spelt correctly.

BURGERS 4U

KING'S KUP KAKES

NOYZE

BEANZ MEANZ HEINZ

EEZEE CLEAN

SUPA KWIK FOTOS

LIGHT BITES

NOYZE MORE STUFF.

Sometimes shops and advertisers deliberately spell words incorrectly to gain attention. Look. This shop's name is really 'Noise'.

LANGUAGE STUDY

● Standard and non-standard English ●

Here is a piece of writing about John Logie Baird. It has been written by a child in non-standard English.

John Logie Baird was the bloke who invented the telly. When he got cheesed off with his job as an engineer he started inventing things. His first inventions were rubbish and all flopped. By the time he was 35 he was broke. He'd lost all his lolly. He scrounged some cash from his mates and had a go at making a machine to send pictures. In 1926 he finally cracked it, and made the first telly.

1 *Rewrite it in standard English as you might find it in a reference book. Do it like this:*

John Logie Baird was the man who invented television.

2 *Write about why you think books are often written in standard English.*

● Slang ●

Write how you think these things would be said in standard English. Do it like this:

a) Would you like to be hit on the nose?

a) D'you want a punch up the bracket?

b) What a load of rubbish!

c) Who's pinched me pen?

d) Let's scarper quick.

e) Oi! You've dropped a quid.

f) Me and Sam watched the footie on telly.

Standard English is the language you expect to find in most printed books. It is often used in writing. People like the news readers on TV would use it. Many people regard it as 'correct' English.

Non-standard English is the sort of language we might use informally when talking to our friends.

When we're talking we often use slang (words and phrases that are not standard English).

---

extra

Write some slang words you might use for these:

a) money

b) the police

c) someone who tells lies

d) something which is very good

e) hitting someone

WRITING WORKSHOP

● Writing a letter ●

Here's a letter of complaint I sent to the manager of Noyze.

19 Victoria Terrace
Surbiton
Surrey
KT6 9RX

Dear Sir,
I wish to complain about the treatment I received at your store recently and the faulty nature of a TV set you sold me.

Firstly I was very upset by the rude way one of your assistants served me. She continually chewed gum and was more interested in the music programme on TV than in helping me. She actually called me an old fusspot when I complained.

I did buy a Fergus TV set from you but found, when I got it home, that it had no plug and the volume knob had dropped off. When I did plug the set in there was a smell of burning and a flash of smoke. Then the set blew up!

I look forward to your prompt reply.

Yours faithfully,
Albert Smith

Note how Albert has written his address and postcode.

Albert has forgotten to put the date!

Albert has set out the letter clearly in paragraphs.

When you finish a letter end it with either
• *Yours faithfully* (to people whose name you don't know at all)
• *Yours sincerely* (to people you know and want to be polite to)
• *Love from* (to friends and relatives).

I don't want any bad publicity. Help me write a polite letter to Albert Smith in reply to his complaints. Set it out neatly in your book.

Ideas for other letters you could write:

• Write to a friend who has just moved giving them the latest gossip.

• Write to the editor of a local paper about something that bothers you.

• Write to Father Christmas to persuade him he needs your help!

• Write and get information for a school project you are doing.

extra

Draw an envelope in your book and address it correctly for Albert.

52

Advantages and ● disadvantages of TV ●

★ *Copy this chart in your book.*

★ *Write at least four advantages and four disadvantages of television.*

advantages	disadvantages
TV helps you to relax.	

● Types of TV programmes ●

Write the names of two programmes for each category.

● **QUIZ SHOWS**   ● **ADVENTURE PROGRAMMES**   ● **SOAPS**

● **MUSIC**   ● **DOCUMENTARIES**   ● **NEWS**

● **CHAT SHOWS**   ● **CARTOONS/COMEDY SHOWS**   ● **SPORT**

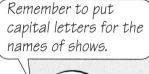

Remember to put capital letters for the names of shows.

● Being a TV critic ●

Think of a TV programme you really enjoyed recently. Use these headings to write a review of it.

- Name of programme
- Channel shown on and time, day and date of broadcast.
- Age, or type, of person the programme was aimed at.
- Details of what the programme was about.
- Characters or places in the programme.
- The thing you particularly liked about the programme.
- Any suggestions for improving the programme.
- Any other comments.

A **critic** is someone who looks for **good** and **bad** points about things.

You watch too much TV. We're going to limit your viewing!

● Limiting your viewing ●

- Imagine you were only able to watch TV for five hours a week.
- Decide which programmes you would watch.
- Design a timetable for a week's viewing.
- Set it out, giving the day, time and how long each programme lasts.
- Give a reason for selecting each programme.

MANY PEOPLE think giants are the original inhabitants of the earth. People think of giants as being like the giant in *Jack and the Beanstalk* who was half human and half monster – cruel, huge, strong and nasty. Giants are often portrayed as slow and stupid.

One Norse legend features a hero called Beowulf and his battle with an enormous bad-tempered ogre called Grendel. This giant used to attack King Hrothgar, capture several men, carry them back to his lair and devour them. In the story, the brave Beowulf came to the rescue and agreed to slay the giant for the king. After an incredible fight Beowulf eventually defeated and killed Grendel.

Some people believe there are still giants alive today. One unsolved modern mystery is the existence of the Yeti. In the Himalayan mountains reliable witnesses claim to have seen this creature, which is often known as the Abominable Snowman. It is said to be a cross between a huge human being and an ape. Also, in America several sightings have been made of the Bigfoot which is said to be up to three metres tall and, judging by the footprints, to weigh around 225 kilos. The Bigfoot is supposed to be rather like a human being, walking upright, its body covered with shaggy brown hair.

COMPREHENSION

● Starting points ●

1 Describe how most people think of giants.

2 Who was Grendel?

3 Whose men did he carry off and eat?

4 What was the name of the hero who slayed Grendel?

5 Write another name for the Yeti.

6 Describe what Bigfoot is supposed to be like.

● Moving on ●

1 Imagine a very different sort of giant. Write a paragraph about a friendly, gentle giant.

2 What do you think are the advantages and disadvantages of being a giant?

3 Do you believe giants still exist? Explain your answer.

4 What do the following words mean:

    a) portrayed   **b**) ogre   **c**) reliable

Use a dictionary to help if you are not sure.

54

STUDY SKILLS

● Main ideas ●

Which of these is the main idea of:

1 Paragraph 1?
   a) Jack and the Beanstalk   **b**) What people think of giants

2 Paragraph 2?
   a) Norse legends   **b**) Beowulf
   c) The story of King Hrothgar

3 Paragraph 3?
   a) Are there still giants today?   **b**) The Yeti   **c**) Bigfoot

extra

Write a passage of three paragraphs. Give it the title 'Three of my favourite possessions'.

● Making notes ●

If you read only the underlined words you can still make sense of the paragraph.

> Many <u>people think giants</u> are the <u>original inhabitants</u> of the <u>earth</u>. People <u>think</u> of <u>giants</u> as being like the giant in Jack and the Beanstalk who was <u>half human</u> and <u>half monster</u>, <u>cruel</u>, <u>huge</u>, <u>strong</u> and <u>nasty</u>. Giants are often portrayed as <u>slow</u> and <u>stupid</u>.

ⓘ When you make notes only write the important words. Leave out all the small words you don't need.

1 *Write out the second paragraph on page 54 again. Underline all the important words.*

2 *Read the third paragraph on page 54 again. In your book, make a note of all the important words in it.*

Do it like this: People believe still giants today.

Read the paragraph you have written. Check that it makes sense.

● Writing from notes ●

Make these notes into proper sentences in your book.

> Giants today? Problem - difference between giant and tall person unclear. TV basketball players up to 2 metres 20 cm tall. Giants or just very tall? Few people suffer gigantism. Gigantism rare disease. Makes people grow very tall. Don't live long. Robert Wadlow grew to height 260cm. Had many problems including brittle bones, difficulty walking.

55

WORD STUDY

● Words ending in 'air' and 'are' ●

Some of these words have been spelt incorrectly. Write out each word correctly with its meaning.

lair	scair	care	chair
dair	glare	repare	rare

These words may have either ending:

fare	hare	stare	pare
fair	hair	stair	pair

Write some sentences including these words showing you understand their meanings.

> Check the spellings of the words in a dictionary if you are not sure.

● Sort out the 'i before e' words ●

Copy these words and complete them with either 'ie' or 'ei'.

1 misch __ __ f
2 retr __ __ ve
3 rec __ __ ve
4 sh __ __ ld
5 n __ __ ce
6 c __ __ ling
7 f __ __ rce
8 dec __ __ ve
9 bel __ __ ve
10 conc __ __ t
11 p __ __ ce
12 th __ __ f

> 'i before e except after c' is quite a good rule to remember.
>
> 'i' usually comes before 'e' in words where the letters make an 'ee' sound, as in th*ie*f but when it follows 'c' it's the other way round, as in rec*ei*ve.

Write some sentences and use these words in them.

science	ancient
sufficient	conscience

> The **'i before e except after c'** rule doesn't always work. Here are a few words that don't follow the rule!

56

LANGUAGE STUDY

● Possessive pronouns ●

Complete each of these sentences in your book using a possessive pronoun.

1 The dog belongs to him. It is _____ .
2 Does the hamster belong to her? Is it _____ ?
3 I saw you drop this pen. I think it must be _____ .
4 This football belongs to us. It's _____ .
5 "This comic belongs to me. I saw it first so it must be _____ ," the girl said.
6 I really like the Smiths' photos. I think _____ are the best.

● I or me? ●

Write these sentences in your book. Use either 'I' or 'me' to complete them.

1 Sam and ____ went to the shops.
2 Jane took a photo of Mark and _____ .
3 Raza and ____ had to stay in to finish our work.
4 Umayr shouted at Sam and _____ to get out of the way.
5 Ben and ____ won the race easily.
6 The teacher gave the prize to Shiva and _____ .

 Instead of saying **'belongs to me'** we can say **'mine'**. This is a **possessive pronoun**.

POSSESSIVE PRONOUNS

mine, yours, his, hers, its, ours, theirs.

The Cover-up test

If you don't know whether to use 'I' or 'me',

Cover up the other person and see which it should be!

~~Ben and~~ me won.

~~Ben and~~ I won.

57

WRITING WORKSHOP

● Indirect speech ●

Direct speech:
Miss Smith said, "Stop throwing things, Raza!'

Indirect speech:
Miss Smith told Raza to stop throwing things.

> **Direct speech** is the words people actually say. We put these words inside speech marks.
>
> **Indirect speech** is when the author tells us roughly what was said, but does not use speech marks.

1 *Change these sentences to indirect speech.*

   a) "Have you seen my slippers, Ben?" Dad asked.

   Dad asked if Ben had seen his slippers.

   b) "Take three pills every day," the doctor told Mr Shah.

   c) "These bananas are not ripe," Mrs Brown complained.

   d) "Help!" shouted the drowning boy.

   e) "It's raining too hard to go out," the teacher said.

2 *Change these sentences to direct speech.*

   a) The teacher asked Emily if she had done her homework.

   "Have you done your homework, Emily?" the teacher asked.

   b) Grandma said that she felt tired.

   c) Rachel told her mum that she had fallen in the mud.

   d) The spy whispered that it was very quiet in the house.

   e) John explained to the policeman that he was lost.

● Calligrams ●

Choose some of these words and make up some calligrams of your own.

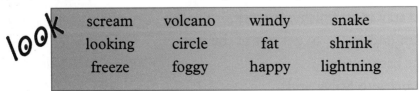

scream	volcano	windy	snake
looking	circle	fat	shrink
freeze	foggy	happy	lightning

> **Calligrams** are ways of drawing words so the shape of them gives us an idea of what the words mean.

● The Wolf's Tale ●

Everyone tells the story from Red Riding Hood's point of view. Read this paragraph and finish the story, telling how I saw things!

As it was such a lovely sunny day, I thought I'd go for a prowl through the woods to see what I could catch for my supper. My ears pricked up as I heard a slight rustling sound in the nearby clearing. Without a sound I crept towards the cover of a bush and peered through the branches. What I saw made my mouth water with anticipation. There, kneeling on the grass picking flowers, was a girl dressed in a red cloak and hood.

i When writing stories it is important to try to think like the **characters**, and to imagine how they would feel and behave. We call this **characterisation**.

● Ways of looking at ... a cuddly toy ●

It's just a bundle of stuffing.

I tell it my secrets.

It stares with glass eyes, wishing it could speak.

It's something to drag around by the ears.

It will always love me.

It never gets jealous.

extra

Tell the story of Jack and the Beanstalk from the giant's point of view.

Choose one of these (or you may decide on something else):

> a teddy   a pet   a television   school

- In rough, try to write down ten or so different ways of looking at it.
- Choose your five or six favourite sentences.
- Make sure there are no silly spelling mistakes.
- Write them out neatly, one under the other, like a poem.
- Give your work a title and illustrate it.

extra

Write a 'Ways of looking at ... ' poem about the Loch Ness Monster!

STUDY SKILLS

1 Write four facts about your favourite crisps. Do not state any personal opinions.

2

Read this paragaph.

> Many hospitals have blood banks. In them, blood of all types is stored. When some blood is needed for an operation, it is taken from the bank. Healthy people give blood to the bank to replace blood that is used. Blood can be kept refrigerated for about three weeks. A chemical is added to the blood to prevent it from clotting.

a) Think of a good title for the paragraph.

b) Make some short notes on the paragraph.

WORD STUDY

1 Copy these words.

listen	scent	castle	guild
scene	guess	rustle	biscuit
guard	muscle	science	whistle

Circle any silent c's.

Underline any silent t's.

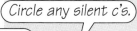

2 Rewrite these words. Insert the letters you think are missing.

a) __ __ ost

b) __ __ ysical

c) d __ __ mond

d) rad __ __

e) f __ __ rly

f) bew __ __ re

g) rec __ __ ve

h) th __ __ f

Cross out any silent u's.

60

LANGUAGE STUDY

1 *Complete these sentences with suitable subjects or objects.*

a) _____ hoot.   **b)** _____ blows.

c) The snooker player hit _____ .

d) The angry alsatian chased _____ .

e) _____ fly.   **f)** _____ flashes.

g) The gardener mowed _____ .

2

Match up these colloquialisms with their meanings. Write them in your book.

a wet blanket	useless
at a loose end	paying attention
good for nothing	conceited
stuck up	a discouraging person
hard up	nothing to do
all ears	short of money

3 *Finish these sentences with a suitable personal pronoun.*

a) This toothbrush belongs to me. It is _____ .

b) I found this book. Is it _____ ?

c) Does this bag belong to Tess? Is it _____ ?

WRITING WORKSHOP

Write these sentences in your book. Put in the missing commas.

1 *Find the missing commas.*

a) In the wood I saw a squirrel a fox an owl a badger and a hedgehog.

b) Mrs Smith an old lady down our street fell over on the ice.

c) A month is made up of weeks days hours minutes and seconds.

d) The man who had just come in looked very cross.

2 *In your book, draw an envelope and address it correctly to your Head Teacher, using your school address.*

3 *Rewrite these sentences. Change them into indirect speech.*

a) "What's the weather like?" Ben asked.

b) "Turn right at the end of the road," the policeman told the stranger.

c) The bus driver shouted, "I can't stop!"

d) "My toy's broken," Raza cried.

How the world began

IN THE BEGINNING the world had no shape. There was no sky and no earth. There were no living creatures and no plants. Everywhere was dark and gloomy. The universe was like a huge hen's egg. Inside the egg, in the dark silence, Pan Gu lay curled up in a dark sleep. Pan Gu slept for 18,000 years. Then very slowly he began to wake. The only noise was the sound of his own breathing. Gradually he opened his eyes, but all around him was darkness. This made him furious, and he punched and kicked angrily. There were great cracking sounds as he broke the shell of the egg.

The dark confusion began to separate. Some parts began to float upwards, and heavy things sank downwards. Pan Gu's tantrum had caused the sky to separate from the earth. Soon there was light so that he could see. Pan Gu was pleased.

But the earth and the sky were still too near each other, and he was afraid they would get confused again. So, with his feet firmly on the ground, Pan Gu pushed the sky upwards, away from the earth, with his strong shoulders. For the next 18,000 years, Pan Gu grew taller and lifted the sky further from the earth. He stood, like a tall pillar, using all his strength to support the sky. Only when the sky was many thousands of kilometres from the earth was he satisfied that they would never become mixed up again. Exhausted by his task, the gigantic Pan Gu collapsed. He knew that he was dying, and his last breaths became the winds and the clouds. He let out a few tired grunts and they became the thunder.

Before he died, Pan Gu wanted to make the world more beautiful. His body changed into mountains and his hands and feet became their peaks. His massive muscles became the fields. His blood flowed and became the rivers. The skin and hairs of his body became the forests and flowers. His teeth and bones sank below the ground to become rocks and precious stones. What about the sky? His long hair and beard floated up and became the stars which we see twinkling at night. His sweat and tears changed into the rain which falls to nourish the trees and flowers. His eyes flew up into the sky. One eye became the moon, and the other the sun.

Shui Yuan-ming and Stuart Thompson

COMPREHENSION

● Starting points ●

1 What was like a 'huge hen's egg'?

2 Who was asleep inside the egg?

3 Why did Pan Gu get angry when he first woke?

4 When was Pan Gu satisfied that the sky was high enough?

5 Why did Pan Gu become exhausted?

● Moving on ●

1 Describe what you imagine Pan Gu to be like.

2 Write what the following words mean:
- **a**) tantrum
- **b**) confused
- **c**) exhausted

3 Write some things you liked about the story.

4 Why do you think many cultures and religions have creation stories like this?

STUDY SKILLS

● Abbreviations ●

Match up each abbreviation in Box A with the word it stands for in Box B. Write them out in your book like this:

> hr. = hour

A
n.	vb.	adv.	adj.	hr.
yr.	min.	vol.	temp.	no.

B
adjective	hour	volume	number	verb
year	hour	minute	temperature	adverb

Use a dictionary to help if you are not sure.

What other abbreviations do you know? Write them in your book and write the words they stand for, like this: rd. = road.

Abbreviations are shortened words. They can save time and make writing notes easier.

extra

Find out and write down what each of these stand for:

a) e.g.   **b)** n.b.

c) i.e.   **d)** etc.

e) RSVP **f)** PTO

WORD STUDY

● Adjectives ending in 'ous' and 'ious' ●

Match up the adjective which comes from each noun. Write them in pairs in your book.

Nouns	Adjectives
fame	victorious
danger	suspicious
marvel	famous
disaster	gracious
victory	disastrous
mystery	spacious
fury	mysterious
space	furious
suspicion	dangerous
grace	marvellous

extra

1 Make up a rule explaining what happens to nouns ending in 'y' when changed into adjectives.

e.g. fury - furious

2 Choose five of the adjectives from the box and make up some sentences to include them.

● The surprising sound of 'ch' ●

Write this list of words in two sets according to the way the 'ch' is pronounced.

echo	machine	anchor	choir
chef	stomach	chemist	parachute
ache	brochure	champagne	character

'ch' says 'k'	'ch' says 'sh'
echo	*machine*

extra

1 Write the 'ch' words in alphabetical order.

2 Write the meaning of each word.

LANGUAGE STUDY

● Clauses ●

subject	verb		subject	verb
The clown	tumbled over.		The children	laughed.

Clause 1 **conjunction** **Clause 2**

| The clown tumbled over | (and) | the children laughed. |

Copy these sentences into your book.
Draw a box around each of the two clauses.
Draw a ring around the conjunction.

> The sentence is now made up of two **clauses**. Each clause has its own **subject** and **verb**.

1. It rained hard so we ran under the tree.
2. I was upset because my dad laughed at me.
3. The driver hooted but the sheep just walked slowly.
4. The dog barked when he jumped up.
5. The monkeys climbed the tree after the alligator chased them.

> **i** Every sentence has its own **subject** and **verb**.
>
> We can join the two sentences by adding a **conjunction** (a joining word).

● Who or which? ●

Join the pairs of sentences together with either who *or* which. *Do it like this:*

1. Sam is a tall girl. She is good at netball.
   Sam is a tall girl who is good at netball.
2. I stroked the cat. It was rather fat.
   I stroked the cat which was rather fat.
3. Raza looked at the sky. It was very cloudy.
4. Mrs Shah thanked the children. They did her shopping for her.
5. The caretaker cleaned the classroom. It was very untidy.

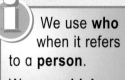

> **i** We use **who** when it refers to a **person**.
>
> We use **which** when it refers to an **animal** or **thing**.

Now use who *or* which *to join the sentences like this:*

6. The man could not hear. He was a little deaf.
   The man, who was a little deaf, could not hear.
7. The tyre had a puncture. It was flat.
8. The dog ate all the food. The dog was very hungry.
9. The girl threw the ball to the boy. She had a blue T-shirt.
10. Khayyam's scarf was lovely and warm. It was bright red.

WRITING WORKSHOP

● Apostrophes showing possession ●

Complete the following in your book:

1  This bike belongs to Mike.

It is Mike's bike.

2  This hat belongs to the clown.

_____

3  This pen belongs to the teacher.

_____

4  This hammer belongs to the builder.

_____

the robbers' car

Now complete these in your book.

5 The car of the robbers   *the robbers' car*

6 The nest of the wasps   _____

7 The burrow of the rabbits   _____

8 The tails of the cats   _____

> **i** In the old days if a boy wrote his name in his book he would write:
>
> *Edward Blake, his book*
>
> Today we write it like this:
>
> *Edward Blake's book*
>
> The **apostrophe** (') shows that **hi** is missing.

> **i** If the there is **more than one** owner, and the plural ends in **s** put the apostrophe **after** the s.

66

● Advertising ●

There were no advertisements in my time! They just try to persuade you to buy things. They often only tell you about the good things and not the bad.

The real facts

* The sweets are expensive.
* You pay a lot for just the wrapping.
* There's not much goodness in them.
* They are made of artificial colours and flavours.
* They are bad for the teeth.

CRUNCHY CRACKLES

The **NEW** sweet sensation

✳ Exciting new colours ✳

Strawberry Purple Orange

★ *Exciting new tastes*
★ **Strawberry Sizzle**
★ *Purple Pop*
★ **Orange Sherbet**

Crunch them!
Munch them!
Feel them

Pop!   **Crackle!**   Crunch!

Fizzle!   **WOP!**

a *SENSATION* you **mustn't** miss

— Interesting name

— NEW = exciting, the latest (Notice the use of capitals to make it stand out.)

— Makes the sweet sound special

— Catchy jingle or rhyme

— Makes the appeal personally to you

Here is a new packet of crisps.

• Make up a name for the product.
• Write a list of the things about the crisps you would not tell people.
• Design an advert to persuade people to buy your crisps.

extra

Write about your favourite advertisement. Say why you like it. What would make you buy the product?

Dahl, Roald
Born 1916 in Llandaff, Wales
An outstandingly popular author of books for children
Died 1990 aged 74

Roald Dahl's early life was almost as adventurous as any of his novels. He did not always enjoy boarding school, finding the teachers there too strict. So it was a relief to leave in order to go out to Africa as a young business man working for Shell Oil. After some extraordinary adventures, some involving wild animals, Dahl volunteered for the Royal Air Force when Britain declared war on Germany in 1939. After flying in East Africa, he crashed his plane in flames in the middle of the Western Desert. Despite dreadful injuries, Dahl was soon flying again in Greece and Syria, before transferring to the USA in 1943.

After World War II he started writing stories, at first for adults and later for children. His third book for children, *Charlie and the Chocolate Factory*, is still one of the best-selling children's books of all time. Other favourites include *The BFG*, *Revolting Rhymes* and *The Witches*. He often used magic in his stories, but in a bold and new way. Sometimes Dahl's stories may seem cruel, at other times even rather rude. But many would say he got closer to what children are interested in than do other more restrained authors writing for the young. Some adults do not like everything he wrote, but young readers themselves seem to. During the 1980s he was the most popular children's author in the world.

From Oxford Children's Encyclopedia

COMPREHENSION

● Starting points ●

Say if these statements are 'true', 'false' or 'not possible to say'.

1 Roald Dahl was happy at school.

2 He joined the Royal Air Force in 1939.

3 Roald Dahl drove a tank in the war.

4 He only wrote stories for children.

5 In the 1980s Roald Dahl was the most popular children's author.

6 Roald Dahl was born in Scotland and died in 1991.

● Moving on ●

1 Give some reasons why you think Roald Dahl might have started writing books for children.

2 Why do you think some adults don't like his books?

3 How could you find the names of some other books Roald Dahl has written?

4 Write the name of an author whose books you have enjoyed. Say what you like about this author's style (the way they write).

extra

Write the titles of five other books Roald Dahl has written.

STUDY SKILLS

● Using an encyclopedia index ●

MANDARIN DUCK Chinese kind of duck with brilliant plumage 6−161b.
MANDARIN ORANGE see Tangerine.
MANDATE order given by League of Nations for Britain and other countries to govern the colonies that had once belonged to Germany and Turkey 10−198a
MANDVILLE Sir John the name used by a writer of fantastic travel tales, written in French and published in the 14th century 3−137b.
MANDINGOS important group of West African Negro tribes, mostly pagan but some Moslems 8−9b.
MADOLIN small stringed musical instrument of the lute family. Where it came from and how it compares with the banjo and the guitar 11−68a; flute family 11−18a.
MANDRAKE poisonous plant related to the potato. The strange shape of the mandrake and legands about it 11−68a.
MANDRILL see Baboon.
MANED WOLF member of the dog tribe, not a true wolf 19−169b.
MANET (manay). Edouard (1832-1883) French painter. How his pictures were little appreciated during his life time 11−68b; 13−39b; impressionists 9−187a; "The Bar at the Folies Bergere", *painting* 11−69.

- subject
- alternative suggestion
- brief information
- volume number
- page number
- column number
- other places to look
- how to pronounce it

(from Encyclopaedia Britannica)

Use this information from an encyclopedia index to answer these questions.

1 Where exactly would you find information on the Maned Wolf?

2 What is a Mandarin Duck?

3 In which two places would you find information on the mandolin?

4 What would you find in volume 3, page 137 column b?

5 Write how you would pronounce the name of Manet.

6 In what order are the subjects listed in the index?

WORD STUDY

● Words ending in 'ary', 'ery' and 'ory' ●

*Copy these words into your book. Finish them with either 'ary', 'ery'
or 'ory'. Use a dictionary to check if you are not sure.*

1 ordin ☐   2 mem ☐

3 cook ☐   4 machin ☐

5 st ☐   6 bound ☐

7 robb ☐   8 necess ☐   9 fact ☐

10 diction ☐   11 secret ☐   12 myst ☐

13 vict ☐   14 hist ☐   15 brav ☐

● Words ending in 'ent' and 'ence' ●

Copy and complete this chart in your book.

Adjectives	Nouns
violent	violence
	silence
confident	
	difference
absent	
obedient	
	evidence
	intelligence
magnificent	

extra

*Write two
sentences to
show the
difference
between
'stationary' and
'stationery'.*

i The endings
'ent' and 'ence'
are more common
than 'ant' and
'ance'.

extra

*Write the **nouns**
that come from
these 'ant'
adjectives e.g.
distant - distance*

*important
ignorant
elegant
fragrant
defiant*

LANGUAGE STUDY

● Idioms ●

> *People say some funny things sometimes!*

To let the cat out of the bag really means to give away a secret!

> **Idioms** are unusual ways of saying things. The real meaning has little to do with the meaning of the words used!

Match the idioms with what you think they mean.

1 To have a bone to pick   *To make a fresh start*
2 To have green fingers   *To get into trouble*
3 To sit on the fence   *To have a complaint to make*
4 To turn over a new leaf   *To own up if you've done wrong*
5 To smell a rat   *To keep something a secret*
6 To get into hot water   *To be good at growing things*
7 To keep it dark   *To be suspicious*
8 To face the music   *To avoid taking sides*

> **extra**
>
> *Draw some funny pictures to accompany your answers.*

● Proverbs ●

Look before you leap really means to think before you act.

Write what you think these proverbs mean.

1 Make hay while the sun shines.
2 Every cloud has a silver lining.
3 Empty vessels make most noise.
4 Birds of a feather flock together.
5 Don't count your chickens before they are hatched.
6 One man's meat is another man's poison.

> A **proverb** is a short, wise saying which has been in common use for many years.

> **extra**
>
> *1 Write down any other proverbs you have heard.*
>
> *2 See what you can find out about the Book of Proverbs in the Bible.*

71

WRITING WORKSHOP

● Joining sentences ●

1 *Find ways of making each of these into* <u>one</u> *sentence.*

a) Ben has hurt his hand. He can't write.
Ben can't write because he has hurt his hand.

b) Sam has a good voice. She sings in the school choir.
Sam, who has a good voice, sings in the school choir.

c) Mrs Smith lost her book. She was on her way to the library.

d) Mark opened the cupboard. He was amazed to find lots of toys in it.

e) The farmer was riding a horse. It looked rather old.

You may have to add or leave out some words. Here are a couple of examples to help you.

2 *Now try these. Do them like this:*

a) I crept up behind Shanaz. I made her jump.
Creeping up behind Shanaz, I made her jump.

b) Shireen heard a footstep behind her. She turned around quickly.

c) The girl screamed with horror. She ran out of the room.

d) Jo looked out of the window. She saw a van draw up.

e) A man got out of the van. He came up the path.

● DIY sentence poem ●

Choose someone you know well or a character from a book you have read. Start by writing a sentence like this:

Charlie won a prize to visit a chocolate factory.

Now add some more sentences to follow on.
Choose some ideas from this list.

Write a sentence that....

1 ... is very short.

2 ... has a wish in it.

3 ... has a colour in it.

4 ... has an emotion in it.

5 ... contains 'looks like'.

6 ... is very long.

7 ... contains 'because'.

8 ... has two adjectives in it.

9 ... contains 'but'.

10 ... ends with an exclamation or question mark.

When you have finished you will have a sentence poem!

● Getting off to a good start ●

Choose one of these story starters to help you begin writing a story.

 *What could go wrong on a quiet Sunday afternoon? There I was, minding my own business, out doing a spot of bird-watching, when suddenly through my binoculars I saw something that made my hair stand on end.*

 *The storm that had battered the coast had died down at last. (Name of character) decided to walk along the coast to see what had been washed up on the shore – and found something that led to a quite unexpected adventure. There, lying on the beach, was an innocent-looking bottle, with something inside it.*

> You must get your audience interested from the start. Here are three opening paragraphs to help you. Remember to give your story an interesting ending too!

The lightning zig-zagged like a jagged spear across the angry sky and ripped into the old oak tree. With a sickening groan the tree split down the middle, revealing (a map? an old chest? a stairway? something else?) which had lain hidden for many years.

• *Before you begin, write yourself a rough plan for your story like this:*

> found old map – thick wood – empty cottage
>
> come across a problem – booby traps guard
>
> the secret – a narrow escape – secret found at last!

> Here is a plan I made for the last idea to show you what to do.

• *Write or word process your story. (It is easier to change things if you are able to do it on a computer!)*

> *Remember…*

  • to include dialogue (things people say).

  • to use interesting adjectives to describe characters and settings.

  • to say how people feel.

  • to start a new paragraph each time something new happens.

  • to check what you have written and see if anything needs changing.

> **i** Look back to page 8 to remind yourself of other things to consider when planning a story.

Giant Thunder

Giant Thunder, striding home,
Wonders if his supper's done.
'Hag wife, hag wife, bring me my bones!'
'They're not done,' the old hag moans.
'Not done? Not done?' the giant roars
And heaves his old wife out of doors.
Cries he, 'I'll have them, cooked or not!'
But overturns the cooking pot.
He flings the burning coals about;
See how the lightning flashes out!
Upon the gale the old hag rides,
The cloudy moon for terror hides.
All the world with thunder quakes;
Forest shudders, mountain shakes;
From the cloud the rainstorm breaks;
Village ponds are turned to lakes;
Every living creature wakes.
Hungry Giant, lie you still!
Stamp no more from hill to hill -
Tomorrow you shall have your fill.

James Reeves

COMPREHENSION

● Starting points ●

Write sentences to answer to these questions.

1 What does the giant want for his supper?

2 What does the giant do to his wife because his supper is
   not ready?

3 What happens when the giant overturns the cooking pot?

4 What does the thunder make the forests and mountains do?

5 What makes the village ponds turn to lakes?

6 Why does every living creature wake up?

● Moving on ●

1 What sort of picture comes into your mind when you read
   this poem? Write a few of your thoughts in your book.

2 Say some things you liked about the poem.

3 There are many violent and loud words in the poem. Write some of them down in your book.

4 The poet isn't really talking about a giant. What is he describing?

STUDY SKILLS

Organising non-fiction books
● The Dewey System ●

Most libraries organise their non-fiction books according to the **Dewey System**. In this system each book is given a number according to the subject it contains. There are ten main subject areas.

This chart shows the main subjects in the Dewey system.

Dewey No.	Subject	Examples
000-099	General Reference	encyclopedias, dictionaries, etc.
100-199	Philosophy	ideas about life
200-299	Religion	world religions, religious leaders
300-399	Social Sciences	hospitals, post office, police, etc.
400-499	Language	English and foreign languages
500-599	Science	maths, chemistry, animals, etc.
600-699	Technology	farming, building, computers, etc.
700-799	The Arts	music, art, dance, sport, etc.
800-899	Literature	stories, poems, plays, etc.
900-999	History, Geography, Biography	people in the past, atlases, countries, etc.

Use the chart to help you answer these questions.

1 In a library, which numbers would you look for to find books about:

a) religion   **b)** music   **c)** poetry   **d)** the police

e) electricity   **f)** history   **g)** French   **h)** computers

2 What main subject would books with these Dewey numbers be about?

a) 600

b) 850

c) 297

d) 925

Explain in writing how the non-fiction books in your school library are organised.

Many libraries have a **subject index** to help you find the topic you are looking for. This is often a card index. It lists the subjects in alphabetical order and gives you the Dewey number of each book.

WORD STUDY

● Same letters but different sounds ●

enough	bought
dough	plough
tough	thought
through	though
bough	rough
fought	although

Say each word and listen to the sound the 'ough' makes.

1 Write the three words where the 'ough' sounds like 'uff' (as in c<u>uff</u>).

2 Write the three words where the 'ough' sounds like 'or' (as in t<u>or</u>n).

3 Write the one word where the 'ough' sounds like 'oo' (as in z<u>oo</u>).

4 Write the two words where the 'ough' sounds like 'ow' (as in n<u>ow</u>).

5 Write the three words where the 'ough' sounds like 'ow' (as in sn<u>ow</u>).

extra

Divide these words into two sets according to the way the 'augh' sounds:

*laugh
caught
naughty
draught
laughter
daughter*

● Pronunciation ●

Say these words and listen to the sound the 'o' makes. Copy them into your book and mark whether the 'o' has a short or a long sound.

1 hope	**2** pot	**3** mother	**4** lose
5 money	**6** wonderful	**7** two	**8** whose
9 improve	**10** above		

Now copy these words and mark whether the 'ou' makes a short or long sound.

1 double	**2** coupon	**3** could	**4** touch
5 young	**6** wound	**7** should	**8** country
9 couple	**10** would		

ⓘ This sign is used in dictionaries to show you that it is a **short** sound - pŏt.

This sign is used to show it is a **long** sound - hōpe.

LANGUAGE STUDY

● Similes ●

1 *Complete these similes in your own words in your book.*

a) as quick as _____   **b**) as tough as _____

c) as soft as _____   **d**) as hot as _____

e) as easy as _____   **f**) as clean as _____

2 *Finish these sentences in your own words with suitable similes.*

a) The smooth sea was like _____

b) The girl could swim like _____

c) The old man snored like _____

d) The puppy raced around like_____

e) The rain crashed down like _____ _

> *Sometimes we describe something by comparing it with another thing. We call these **similes**. e.g. My feet were as cold as an ice lolly. My hands were like icicles.*

● Metaphors ●

The wind is a roaring tiger
that has escaped from the zoo.

1 *Copy these sentences and underline the metaphor in each.*

a) The chimney sends up a black, twisting snake of smoke.

b) I crept quietly downstairs on velvet paws.

c) The dog chased its tail, a spinning whirlpool going round and round.

d) The old man, with a wrinkled lizard's face, smiled to the baby.

e) Anger was an exploding canon going off in my head.

2 *Use your imagination. Think what these things remind you of. Use a metaphor to finish each sentence.*

a) The breeze in the grass is a _____

b) The thick snow is a _____ on the ground.

c) The thick mist was a _____ around us.

d) The stormy sea is a _____

e) The flame from the match is a _____

> *A **metaphor** is like a simile but goes further by saying one thing *is* another. Look and see what metaphors the poet uses in the poem on page 74.*

> ## extra
> *Writers use similes and metaphors to make their writing more interesting. Look through some story and poetry books and note down any similes or metaphors you can spot.*

WRITING WORKSHOP

● Types of sentence ●

a statement   **a question**   **a command**

These are the bones for my dinner.

Where are my bones?

Bring me my bones.

> Sentences do different jobs. You can:
>
> - make a **statement** of fact.
>
> - ask a **question**.
>
> - give a **command** (in which someone is told what to do).

1 *In your book write if these are statements, questions or commands.*

a) I like football.

b) Give me your money.

c) Can I come with you?

d) The dog ate the slipper.

e) Dover isn't in Wales.

f) Where is Aberdeen?

g) Stop messing about.

h) I'll be with you soon.

i) Is the pudding sweet?

j) Boil the eggs for five minutes.

2 *Make these statements into questions.*

a) The Cup Final is played at Wembley.
Is the Cup Final played at Wembley?

b) My name is Rumplestiltskin.

c) The children were playing in the playground.

d) The smell of freshly-baked bread is lovely.

e) The Tyranosaurus Rex was one of the most powerful dinosaurs.

A positive statement   **A negative statement**

These are my slippers.

These are not my slippers.

3 *Change these into negative statements.*

a) Sam likes cricket.

b) The children were making a lot of noise.

c) The holiday begins on Thursday.

d) Eric plays the guitar very well.

e) The monster went home.

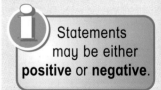

> Statements may be either **positive** or **negative**.

● Using metaphors in poetry ●

THE SUN

The sun is a wheel of fire
Rolling across the sky.
The sun is an orange marigold
Growing in the sky's garden.

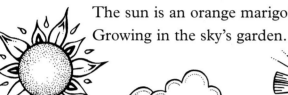

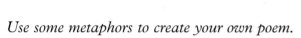

In the poem on page 74 the poet says that thunder is a roaring giant. This short poem on The Sun contains two metaphors.

Use some metaphors to create your own poem.

- Write three verses.
- Use two metaphors in each verse.
- Give each verse a different subject.
- Choose from the subjects on the right for your verses.
- Before doing a final version of your poem....

★ Write your ideas in rough.

★ Add or change anything you don't like.

★ Check your spelling and punctuation.

★ Decide how you want to present your poem:
  - with a decorated border?
  - written on top of a picture?
  - with an illustration for each verse?
  - with a picture at the top or bottom?
  - with no illustrations?

★ Decide on a title.

★ Will it be written in best writing or word processed?

---

the sun

the stars

the moon

rain

fog

lightning

thunder

ice

snow

clouds

Now make a final copy of your finished poem.

The Snow Goose

She had never seen Rhayader before and was close to fleeing in panic at the dark apparition that appeared at the studio door, drawn by her footsteps – the black head and beard, the sinister hump, and the crooked claw. She stood there staring, poised like a disturbed marsh bird for instant flight.

But his voice was deep and kind when he spoke to her. 'What is it, child?'

She stood her ground, and then edged timidly forward. The thing she carried in her arms was a large white bird, and it was quite still. There were stains of blood on its whiteness and on her kirtle where she had held it to her. The girl placed it in his arms. 'I found it, sir. It's hurted. Is it still alive?'

'Yes. Yes, I think so. Come in, child, come in.'

Rhayader went inside, bearing the bird, which he placed upon a table, where it moved feebly. Curiosity overcame fear. The girl followed and found herself in a room warmed by a coal fire, shining with many coloured pictures that covered the walls, and full of a strange, but pleasant smell.

The bird fluttered. With his good hand Rhayader spread one of its immense white pinions. The end was beautifully tipped with black. Rhayader looked at it and marvelled, and said, 'Child, where did you find it?'

'In t'marsh, sir, where fowlers had been. What – what is it, sir?'

'It's a snow goose from Canada. But how in all heaven came it here?'

Paul Gallico

COMPREHENSION

● Starting points ●

Write the missing words in your book.

The girl held the __1__ bird in her arms as she __2__ on Rhayader's door. She was scared at first when the door __3__ and she saw Rhayader, but when he spoke in a __4__ voice she felt a little __5__ . Rhayader __6__ the girl to come in. His room was warmed by a __7__ fire and had a pleasant __8__ . After he had placed the bird on the table it __9__ its wings. Rhayader asked her where she had found it. He told her it was a snow goose from __10__ .

● Moving on ●

1 Write down some of the thoughts that might have been going through the girl's head as she approached Rhayader's door.

2 What sort of man do you think Rhayader was?

3 How can you tell the story took place some years ago?

4 The story says that the girl's curiosity overcame her fear. Write what you think this means.

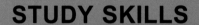

STUDY SKILLS

● Book inspection ●

Choose a fiction and a non-fiction book from your library. Follow the instructions and carry out a book inspection on both books.

The fiction book

1 Write in your book:
   a) the title   b) the author
   c) the publisher   d) its date of publication.

2 Does it have a clear contents page?

3 Are chapter headings clearly marked?

4 Give your opinion of:
   a) the cover illustration   b) the back cover blurb
   c) the use of illustrations in the book.

5 In your opinion, what makes a good fiction book?

The non-fiction book

1 Write in your book:
   a) the title   b) the author
   c) the publisher   d) its date of publication.

2 Does the book have a clear:
   a) contents page   b) index page?

3 Is there a bibliography (a list of further books to read on the topic)?

4 Give your opinion on:
   a) the use of pictures, illustrations and diagrams in the book
   b) the use of headings throughout the book to help you find information easily
   c) page layouts: are pages clearly laid out? are they easy to find your way about?

5 In your opinion, what makes good non-fiction?

WORD STUDY

● Words ending in 'ate, 'ete' and 'ite' ●

> fortunate   athlete
> favourite   educate   illustrate
> delete   polite
> demonstrate   opposite
> desperate   complete   definite
> separate   compete

'ate' is the most common ending of the three.

Read the definitions and write the correct word for each of the following in your book:

1 to draw   _ _ _ _ _ _ _ _ a t e
2 hopeless   _ _ _ _ _ _ _ a t e
3 to divide   _ _ _ _ _ a t e
4 lucky   _ _ _ _ _ _ _ a t e
5 to show   _ _ _ _ _ _ _ _ _ a t e
6 to teach   _ _ _ _ a t e
7 certain   _ _ _ _ _ i t e
8 well-mannered   _ _ _ _ i t e
9 completely different   _ _ _ _ _ _ i t e
10 most liked   _ _ _ _ _ _ _ i t e

Now copy all the 'ete' words from the box into your book and make up a definition for each.

● Words ending in 'ise' ●

> advertise   surprise   realise
> organise   recognise   exercise   apologise
> disguise   supervise   despise

In your book write:

1 the two seven-letter 'ise' words.
2 the four eight-letter 'ise' words.
3 the four nine-letter 'ise' words.

---

extra

Write the meanings of these words:

*translate
dictate
considerate
investigate
decorate
climate
stagnate
recite
exquisite
excite*

---

i 'ise' is more common at the end of words than 'ize'. There are just a few common words ending in 'ize' These are: 'size', 'prize' and 'capsize'. Can you find any more?

LANGUAGE STUDY

● Dialect ●

These two people are both saying the same thing. In your book write what they are saying in standard English.

When I were a little lad.

A man from Lancashire

When I woz a nipper.

A woman from London.

> **i** In different places people have different ways of saying things in English. These words and phrases are called **dialect**.

Write in standard English what this person from Scotland said.

The bairns went to the seaside. They played in a rockpool and looked for wee beasties that bide there.

> **i**
>
> bairns = children
> wee = little
> beasties = creatures
> bide = live

Write out this poem in your best writing. Underline any phrases or words in dialect.

> This is part of a poem written in a form of West Indian dialect.

If it wasn't you
who tek de chalk
and mark up de wall
juggle with de egg
and mek it fall
then why you didn't answer
when you hear Granny call?

If it wasn't you
who bounce yuh ball
in de goldfish bowl
wipe mud from yuh shoes
all over de floor
and poke yuh finger
straight in de butter
if it wasn't you
then why yuh heart a-flutter?

John Agard

> **extra**
>
> *Have a go at writing the poem out in standard English.*

83

WRITING WORKSHOP

● Looking back ●

I have lots of special memories, some good and some not so good.

Choose three of these and write a paragraph about each.

- something that happened when I was very young
- something that made me very happy
- something that made me very sad
- something I found very exciting
- something that was a surprise to me
- something I found very strange
- something that worried me
- something really funny that happened to me

● Looking forward ●

Try to imagine what life will be like when you are fifty!

Write some thoughtful answers to these questions:

- What will you be wearing and where will you live?
- How will you travel around?
- What job will you be doing – or won't you need to work?
- How will you entertain yourself?
- Where will you be going for your holidays?
- Will there still be illness and disease?
- Will there still be hungry people?
- Will some more animals have become extinct?
- Will the world be a better place?

extra

Resolutions

Write down three things you will decide to do differently in the future.

Wishes

Write down three things you wish you could change in the world in the future.

● The Door ●

I wonder what will happen when I knock on the door.

Imagine you are standing in front of a door.

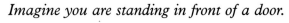

- **What sort of door is it?**

    Is it old? new? wooden? glass? metal? small? huge?

- **Where is it?**

    - in a multi-story block of flats?
    - in a palace?
    - in an old, deserted cottage?
    - in a wall?
    - in a spacecraft?
    - somewhere else?

- **When is it?**

    Now? in the past? in the future?

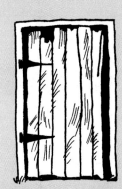

- **It opens –**

    - smoothly? with a creak?
    - into a tunnel?
    - into a different world?
    - into a space ship?
    - somewhere else?

- **What happens?**

*Write a story called '**The Door**'.*

Jabberwocky

'Twas brillig, and the slithy toves
Did gyre and gimble in the wabe;
All mimsy were the borogroves,
And the mome raths outgrabe.

'Beware the Jabberwock, my son!
The jaws that bite, the claws that catch!
Beware the Jubjub bird, and shun
The frumious Bandersnatch!'

He took his vorpal sword in hand:
Longtime the manxome foe he sought -
So rested he by the Tumtum tree,
And stood awhile in thought.

And as in uffish thought he stood,
The Jabberwock, with eyes of flame,
Came whiffling through the tulgey wood
And burbled as it came!

One, two! One, two! And through and through
The vorpal blade went snicker-snack!
He left it dead, and with its head
He went galumphing back.

Lewis Carroll

Although you may not understand all the words, try to answer these questions in your book.

COMPREHENSION

● Starting points ●

1 What sort of 'toves' were they?

2 Where did they 'gyre and gimble'?

3 What were the 'borogroves' like?

4 What sort of sword did the man carry?

5 Which tree did he rest by?

6 What did the Jabberwock do as it came through the wood?

● Moving on ●

1 Write some things you have discovered about the Jabberwock.

2 Do you understand every word in the poem? Does it matter?
Explain your answers.

3 What do you think of the poem? Give your opinion.

STUDY SKILLS

● Using context clues ●

(sharp?) (trusty?) (something else?)

He took his *vorpal* sword in hand.

> **i** We don't have to know every word we read. Often the other words around it help us to guess the meanings of unknown words. This is called **using context clues**.

Write what you think the underlined words mean in these sentences.

1 After the Romans had invaded the country there were only <u>sporadic</u> outbursts of fighting from some tribes.

2 The people of Little Minton were proud of their village, which was a very <u>picturesque</u> spot.

3 When Mrs Jackson told Tom off for not doing his homework he was very <u>piqued</u>.

4 The soldiers built the castle in a good <u>strategic</u> position on top of a hill overlooking the surrounding countryside.

5 When questioned by the police, the thief would not <u>divulge</u> any information about his <u>accomplices</u>.

6 Tess often felt lonely living in one of the <u>scattered</u> farms up in the valley.

7 The fishermen were unhappy with their poor <u>catch</u>.

8 The explorer was <u>frozen to the spot</u> when he came face to face with the polar bear.

87

WORD STUDY

● Serial probability ●

I don't think that looks right!

When spelling we need to understand **serial probability**. We need to know that certain combinations of letters occur in writing and others are not possible.

It was a plessunt day.

1 *Below are some common letter patterns found in English. Write one word containing each pattern.*

a) ice - *notice*		**b)** ough
c) ity		**d)** ure
e) tion		**f)** ite
g) our		**h)** sch
i) cen		**j)** ext
k) ph		**l)** zzle

In each of these groups of nonsense words only one word has a letter pattern that is possible in English.

2 *Write the nonsense word in each group that looks as if it could be an English word.*

a) xepvt	lodl	<u>briller</u>
b) pdjis	wrock	hosm
c) plange	xevis	bcdfe
d) hjomnf	exdence	luknmb
e) imprant	qtesaf	mmksgtreah
f) gimble	bvguiy	fsoplw
g) hough	gotjykh	hdsretpk
h) gwqytup	grould	pnbvquafg

88

LANGUAGE STUDY

● Glossary of useful words ●

Take each word from the Word Box on the right. Match it with one of the definitions below, like this.

Adjective   *A word which describes a noun. It tells us more about it.*

Definitions:

This is a naming word.

This is a word for telling what is happening or what people are doing.

This word is sometimes used instead of a noun.

A word which describes a noun. It tells us more about it.

All the words we know and use.

A word that can be used to join two sentences together.

The study of language.

The kind of English which is most widely understood.

A word which goes with a verb, often saying how, when or where something happened.

Word Box

adjective

adverb

conjunction

grammar

noun

pronoun

standard English

verb

vocabulary

---

extra

*Think of other words you have learnt in this Essential English book (e.g. synonymn, metaphor). Add them to your **Glossary** with their definitions.*

89

WRITING WORKSHOP

● The Jabberwock's song ●

*Look carefully at the poem below, called **The Loch Ness
Monster's Song**. Try to read it with expression.
Use the punctuation marks to help you.*

Sssnnnwhufffll?

Hnwhuffl hhnnwfl hnfl hfl?

Gdroblboblhobngbl gbl gl gg g g g glbgl.

Drublhaflablhaflubhafgabhaflhafl fl fl-

bm grawwww grf grawf awfgm graw gm.

Hovoplodok-doplodovok-plovodokot-doplodokosh?

Splgraw fok fok splgrafhatchgabrlgabrl fok splfok!

Zgra kra gka fok!

Grof grawff gahf?

Gombl mbl bl-

blm plm,

blm, plm,

blm, plm,

blp.

Edwin Morgan

Notice

- how some of the long 'words' contain smaller 'words' in them.

- how lots of the words and letters are repeated.

- how the letters and words make some interesting sounds.

(When we play with the sound of language like this we call it **onomatopoea**.)

*Imagine the Jabberwock was playing in a lake, really enjoying itself,
splashing around and having a good time. Make up a poem like the
one above that it would sing.*

● Story-writing review ●

Throughout the Essential English course we have learnt a lot about story-writing. Let's review some of the facts.

All stories are the same!

In all stories you would expect to find the same sort of things like:

characters (who the story is about)
a setting (where the story takes place)
a storyline (the events that happen)

BUT all stories are also different! You would expect to find **different** types of things in **different** types of stories. Let's look at fairy stories as an example.

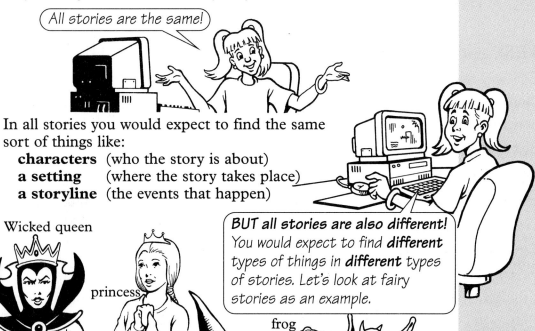

Wicked queen

princess

prince

frog

witch

giant

monster

Types of character
- you might find some of these

castle

woods

palace

cave

Types of setting
- you might find some of these

magic spells

being captured

getting lost

happy endings

Types of event
- you might find some of these

In your book, write the sort of characters, settings and events you might find in one of the following:

| monster stories | space stories | animal stories |

Do you remember? Test 3

STUDY SKILLS

1 *In your book, explain briefly what each of these are:*

a) The Dewey System

b) An author index

c) A glossary

d) a book blurb

e) a contents page

2 *Match up the abbreviations with their meanings.*

R.S.V.P.	established
a.m.	Saint or Street
Dr.	kilometre
est.	please turn over
km.	please reply
min.	United States of America
St.	Doctor
U.S.A.	before noon
P.T.O.	and other things
etc.	minute or minimum

WORD STUDY

1 *Choose 'ous' or 'ious' to complete these words:*

danger ☐   myster ☐   grac ☐   fam ☐

2 *Choose 'ary' or 'ory' or 'ery' to complete these words:*

fact ☐   myst ☐   mem ☐

ordin ☐   necess ☐   brav ☐

> Choose 'ence' or 'ance' to complete the words in number 3.

3   import ☐   confid ☐   viol ☐   ignor ☐

92

4 *Choose 'ete' or 'ate' or 'ite' to complete these words:*

separ ☐   oppos ☐   compl ☐

athl ☐   educ ☐   favour ☐

5 *Choose 'ough' or 'augh' to complete these words:*

t ☐   c ☐   l ☐   d ☐

LANGUAGE STUDY

1 *Copy the sentences. Underline the clauses in each. Circle the conjunction in each.*

> These sentences are made up of two clauses and a conjunction.

  a) The guard dog barked loudly so the burglar ran off.

  b) We had to return home as it rained so hard.

  c) The mouse scuttled for cover when the owl swooped down.

  d) The farmer ploughed the field and spread fertiliser on it.

  e) The racing driver braked hard but couldn't keep on the track.

2 *Complete these sentences with 'who' or 'which'.*

  a) The hairdresser cut my hair _____ was very long.

  b) The driver picked up the child _____ had been knocked over.

  c) I whispered to Sam _____ was sitting next to me.

  d) Mrs Woods marked my book _____ was very untidy.

3 *Copy these sentences. Underline the 'simile' or 'metaphor' in each.*

> Each of these sentences contains either a simile or a metaphor.

  a) The eagle swoops like a flash of lightning.

  b) Snow, a thick white blanket, covered the ground.

  c) The bread was as hard as a brick.

  d) The dew on the grass sparkled like diamonds.

  e) The volcano, a huge angry giant, roared and spat lava.

4 *Write what you think these idioms mean.*

  a) to bury the hatchet   b) to hit below the belt

  c) to be a wet blanket   d) to let the cat out of the bag

93

WRITING WORKSHOP

1 *Copy and complete the following:*

a) the hat belonging to the clown = _the clown's hat_

b) the book belonging to the teacher = _____

c) the thermometer belonging to the nurse = _____

d) the banana belonging to the monkey = _____

e) the shorts belonging to the boys = _____

f) the pens belonging to the girls = _____

g) the den belonging to the foxes = _____

h) the uniforms belonging to the sailors = _____

Now where do I put the apostrophe?

2 *Write a sentence:*

a) that is short.

b) that is long.

c) that ends with a question mark.

d) that ends with an exclamation mark.

e) that contains 'because'.

f) that begins with the word 'stepping'.

g) that begins with the phrase 'the next morning'.

h) that contains the conjunction 'but'.

i) that is a command.

j) that is positive.

k) that is negative.

l) that ends with the phrase 'up the ladder'.

m) that starts with the adverb 'slowly'.

n) that contains the word 'although'.

o) that is a statement of fact.

p) that is a statement of opinion.

q) that contains ten words.

r) that contains two verbs.

IDEAS BANK FOR STORIES

Choose something to write about from these ideas:

Adventures in far-off places
Lost treasure; ancient cities under the oceans or in jungles;
far-away planets and outer space

Adventures around you
Robberies and burglaries; secret clubs and spies;
smugglers; visitors from space; secret doors; strange
disappearances; police and detectives; school stories

Disaster stories
Accidents; being trapped; being kidnapped; fire; gales and
floods

Relationships
Arguments; secrets; broken promises; shocks and surprises;
unexpected visits and unwelcome visitors

Fairy stories
Princesses, wicked queens and handsome princes; giants,
dragons and ogres; caves, woods and mountains; palaces,
castles and cottages

Animal stories
Pets and other domestic animals; adventures with known
wild animals (zoo escapes, jungle/safari tales); unknown
wild animals and creatures (Yeti, Big Foot, Loch Ness
Monster, etc); imagining you are an animal

Time stories
Stories from the past (e.g. prehistoric adventures, I
survived the Fire of London, discovering the pyramids,
etc); science fiction stories from the future (time travel, the
mad inventor, etc.)

Horror stories
Spooky tales; monsters; ghosts; old houses, unexplained
mysteries; tales of the unknown

Throughout this book you have learnt a lot about writing stories. Here are some ideas for you to write about in your own stories.

Remember to look at page 8 to help you with story planning.

extra

Write a book of stories on the same theme.

Make your stories into a book with a proper cover.

Illustrate your stories.

Let others read your stories.

IDEAS FOR CHECKING AND EDITING STORIES

Characters
- Have you described how they look, feel, behave?

Settings
- Have you described the settings well enough?

Story plot
- Does your story have a good beginning, middle, end?
- Can you make it more interesting?
- Do you need to add or move anything?

Punctuation
- Do all your sentences make sense?
- Have you checked your punctuation for: capital letters, full stops, commas, question and exclamation marks, speech marks?

Spelling and handwriting
- Have you checked for silly spelling mistakes?
- Is your handwriting clear and easy to read?

Presentation
- Are you going to print your story on the computer?
- Are you going to illustrate it?
- What format will you present your story in: exercise book, paper, booklet, some other way?